"If you want to be purposeful about making this December more Christ-centered for your children, then look carefully at this little book. Marty Machowski provides the ideas, the plans, and the details: all you have to do is follow his lead. He will help your family have a more gospel-filled Christmas season."

—**Donald S. Whitney,** Professor of Biblical Spirituality, The Southern Baptist Theological Seminary, Louisville, KY; author of *Family Worship: In the Bible, in History, and in Your Home*

"*Prepare Him Room* is a tool to help families focus on Jesus during the Christmas season. Tying together the whole Christmas story from the prophecies concerning Jesus; to his birth, death, and resurrection; culminating in the return of Jesus, Marty Machowski challenges families to celebrate the true meaning of Christmas."

—**Sally Michael,** Cofounder of Children Desiring God; author

"*Prepare Him Room* is one of the best resources I've seen to counter the commercialism, materialism, and sentimentalism that our culture serves up each Christmas. Through Scripture, creative stories, crafts, songs, prayers, and activities, families will be able to reflect on Christ's birth and the gospel with wonder, gratefulness, and joy. It was a privilege to collaborate with Marty on this project, and I can't recommend it highly enough."

—**Bob Kauflin,** Director of Sovereign Grace Music

"*Prepare Him Room* is an endearing, well-conceived, and memory-making resource for the Advent season. Do you want a devotional guide that is certain to become a part of your family's Christmas traditions? Then this is it. More importantly, do you want a devotional guide that links the birth of Christ to Easter and the gospel story in a way that will deepen your family's biblical understanding and bid you prepare him room in your hearts and home this Christmas? Then look no further."

—**Debra Bell, PhD,** Author of the *Ultimate Guide to Homeschooling*

"I have twelve grandchildren who need the gospel, just like their Pop-Pop. That's why I'm so grateful my friend Marty has written *Prepare Him Room*. Parents, these short, simple, and Christ-centered devotionals will help you make the most of the Christmas season as you work to transfer the gospel to the next generation right in your home. May every heart prepare him room, as every home proclaims him as Lord!"

—C. J. Mahaney, Senior Pastor, Sovereign Grace Church of Louisville

"Yet again, Marty Machowski gives us a solid, gospel-centered resource in his new book *Prepare Him Room*. I deeply appreciated the Advent devotionals that consistently pointed to Christ, and my children kept begging me to read the story of Christopher and the Bartimaeus house! In addition, new Advent songs by Bob Kauflin and activities for the children all make this a wonderful resource for every Advent season. Our family will treasure this for years to come."

—Deepak Reju, Pastor of Biblical Counseling and Families, Capitol Hill Baptist Church, Washington, DC; president, Biblical Counseling Coalition; author of *The Pastor and Counseling* and *On Guard: Preventing and Responding to Child Abuse at Church*

PREPARE HIM ROOM

CELEBRATING THE BIRTH OF JESUS
FAMILY DEVOTIONAL

Marty Machowski

WWW.NEWGROWTHPRESS.COM

New Growth Press, Greensboro, NC 27404

Cover/Interior Illustrations: Sarah Bland-Halulko, sarahjbland-halulko.com
Cover/Interior Design and Typesetting: Faceout Books, faceoutstudio.com

ISBN: 978-1-939946-53-9 (Print)
ISBN: 978-1-939946-54-6 (eBook)

Library of Congress Cataloging-in-Publication Data

Machowski, Martin, 1963-
   Prepare Him room : celebrating the birth of Jesus family devotional /
Marty Machowski.
      pages cm
   ISBN 978-1-939946-53-9 (print : alk. paper) -- ISBN 978-1-939946-54-6
(ebook) 1. Advent--Prayers and devotions. 2. Families--Religious life.
I. Title.
   BV40.M335 2014
   249--dc23
                           2014016280
Printed in China

24 23 22 21 20 19 18 17   3 4 5 6 7

CONTENTS

Introduction 1

How to Use This Book 2

Make Your Own Advent Wreath 4

ADVENT WEEK 1

WEEK 1, PART 1. God's Promise: The Hope of a Child 6

WEEK 1, PART 2. The Angel's Announcement: A Visit to Mary 10

WEEK 1, PART 3. The Fulfillment of God's Plan:
Jesus Came in the Fullness of Time 14

Bartimaeus: A Christmas Story, Chapter 1 18

ADVENT WEEK 2

WEEK 2, PART 1. God's Promise: The Greatest Proof of All 24

WEEK 2, PART 2. The Angel's Announcement: Joseph's Dream 28

WEEK 2, PART 3. The Fulfillment of God's Plan: The Word Became Flesh 31

Bartimaeus: A Christmas Story, Chapter 2 35

ADVENT WEEK 3

WEEK 3, PART 1. God's Promise: It Will Happen in Bethlehem 43

WEEK 3, PART 2. The Angel's Announcement: A Visit to the Shepherds 47

WEEK 3, PART 3. The Fulfillment of God's Plan:
The King Was Crowned with Thorns 50

Bartimaeus: A Christmas Story, Chapter 3 54

ADVENT WEEK 4

WEEK 4, PART 1. God's Promise: Salvation Will Come through My Servant 62

WEEK 4, PART 2. Simeon's Announcement:
Welcomed at the Temple 65

WEEK 4, PART 3. The Fulfillment of God's Plan:
People from Every Nation around the Throne 69

Bartimaeus: A Christmas Story, Chapter 4 75

CHRISTMAS DAY CELEBRATION

The Fulfillment of God's Plan: Christ Is Born! 81

INTRODUCTION

Many of the popular Christmas traditions, like stockings hung above the fireplace and blinking lights on fir trees, have little to do with Christ's birth. This book will give you a variety of ways to preserve the real meaning of Christmas by keeping God's Word central in your home.

The word *advent* means "arrival." Advent traditions celebrate the first advent (the birth) of Jesus Christ. These same celebrations view the Christmas story in light of God's larger plan of salvation, looking forward to his second advent (his return) as King. While the virgin birth of Jesus is amazing, what Jesus did in dying on the cross for our sins is the most incredible part of his story. We would have little reason to celebrate apart from the saving work of Jesus on the cross and the anticipation of his return.

Prepare Him Room will take you on an Advent journey, exploring some of the most significant prophecies of the Bible—prophecies that foretold Christ's coming hundreds of years before it happened. Then, it will lead you through the fulfillment of those same prophecies tracing the redemptive plan of God all the way to Christ's second advent. In addition to an Advent Bible study, we've provided activities for your family to enjoy along with a heartwarming Christmas story, "Bartimaeus," to read during the Christmas season.

It is my hope that this book will help your family keep Christ central in your Christmas celebrations and that the gospel truth of Advent will be used by God to transform lives in your family.

HOW TO USE THIS BOOK

This book comprises thirteen family Advent devotionals—three for each of the four weeks of Advent and one more for Christmas—as well as an original Christmas short story called "Bartimaeus: A Christmas Story" for your family to enjoy. Each week, the first devotional explores a significant Old Testament prophecy that foretells the coming of our Savior. The second highlights an announcement of the birth of the Savior or his mission, and the third explores a way the earlier prophecy and announcement have been fulfilled in the life of Christ. The Bartimaeus story unfolds a chapter at a time at the end of each week.

To plan your Advent celebration, after Thanksgiving look at the calendar and take note of the four Sundays before Christmas. These are the days that signal the start of the four weeks of Advent. There are three family Bible devotionals for each of these four weeks. You might want to pick potential days on which to do the devotionals each week. Plan on doing the last study on Christmas Day. Each day features the lyrics of a traditional Christmas carol, in addition to several new songs, that follow the theme of that week's devotions. The companion CD, *Prepare Him Room: Celebrating the Birth of Jesus in Song*, includes the new songs, as well as updated arrangements and new verses to some of the older carols for you to enjoy and sing with your family throughout the Christmas season. Also available for your church is a four-lesson Sunday school curriculum called *Prepare Him Room: Celebrating the Birth of Jesus in the Classroom*. The curriculum covers the same Bible passages on Sunday that you are exploring with your family during the week.

Instructions are included on how to make and incorporate an Advent wreath into your family times. The Advent wreath consists of a simple circle of evergreens. It represents our hope of eternal life in Christ. The four outer candles mark the four Sundays of Advent. These four candles represent the light of God reaching the world through the birth of his son Jesus. In the center of the wreath is placed a fifth, larger, candle that represents the Savior, marking his place at the center of God's plan.

Prior to Advent, purchase an Advent wreath or the supplies to make your own with the instructions we've provided. Then, beginning on the first Sunday in Advent, start your first week's devotional by lighting an Advent candle. After you read the listed Scripture, you will find a short commentary along with discussion questions. End the devotional for the day by praying and singing a Christmas hymn. Follow the same pattern for each devotion. Finally, on Christmas Day, read the Christmas story from Luke's gospel, light the center candle of your Advent wreath, and sing "Joy to the World."

Also, procure a manger scene, preferably one that can be handled by your children. This is helpful in visualizing the details of Christ's birth and adds to the anticipation and impact of the Advent celebration. If your church is using the *Prepare Him Room* Sunday school curriculum, your younger grade school children will be making their own stable and manger with all the traditional figures as a craft within the classroom lessons.

Before you begin...

MAKE YOUR OWN
ADVENT WREATH

Making your own Advent wreath is an easy family project. If you have the companion CD, *Prepare Him Room: Celebrating the Birth of Jesus in Song*, this is a good time to turn it on and start familiarizing yourself with the songs you'll be singing throughout the devotional.

SUPPLIES NEEDED:

* ✱ 96" (8 feet) evergreen roping—real or artificial
* ✱ 16" diameter green foam ring
* ✱ three 10" purple taper candles (you can substitute white candles here)
* ✱ one 10" pink taper candle (you can substitute a red candle)
* ✱ one 2"x 6" white pillar candle with holder or white jar candle

* aluminum foil, heavy duty
* knife or apple corer
* hot glue gun

INSTRUCTIONS: Lay the foam ring on a protected work surface. With the sharp knife or apple corer, cut out four holes in the ring equal distances apart to accept the four taper candles. Be careful to cut the holes slightly smaller than the candle diameter. Hot glue the candles into the holes making sure they are perfectly vertical. Wrap the evergreen roping along the foam ring gluing it to the ring as you go. The 8-foot length should be plenty to cover the outer and inner circumferences of the foam ring. The goal is to cover the ring completely. Set your wreath on a table and place the pillar candle in the center. Remember to protect the surface of the table underneath the wreath from dripping wax.

God's Promise:
The Hope of a Child

SUPPLIES NEEDED:
* ∗ recording of Handel's *Messiah* (YouTube has several options)
* ∗ crayons, markers, paints, etc.
* ∗ white paper

WARM-UP
Listen to Handel's Oratorio, Messiah

—Play a recording of the chorus, "For Unto Us a Child Is Born" from Handel's *Messiah*. Ask your children to listen carefully to see if they can pick out some of the names of Jesus.

—At the end of this session play a recording of the "Hallelujah" chorus from *Messiah*.

READ THE PROPHECY
Light the first Advent candle and then read the Scripture below.

For to us a child is born, to us a son is given; and the government shall be upon his shoulder, and his name shall be called Wonderful Counselor, Mighty God, Everlasting Father, Prince of Peace. Of the increase of his government and of peace there will be no end, on the throne of David and over his kingdom, to establish it and to uphold it with justice and with righteousness from this time forth and forevermore. The zeal of the Lord of hosts will do this. (Isaiah 9:6-7)

PICTURE IT

Isaiah spoke his prophecy to the people of Israel in a time when they were disobeying God. Isaiah brought terrible warnings telling them that God would take away their food and water and bring enemies against them. But in chapter nine, Isaiah gave God's people a promise of hope: In spite of their great sin, God would take their sadness away.

In verse six of chapter nine, Isaiah described this promised hope as the coming of a very special child. The child would be both man and God and would rule forever and ever in peace over God's people. Isaiah's wonderful prophecy declared that the child would be called "Wonderful Counselor, Mighty God, Everlasting Father, Prince of Peace."

Almost three centuries ago, George Frideric Handel wrote a long musical composition to celebrate God's prophecy through Isaiah to his people. This famous Christmas promise—that God would send his Son, Jesus—are the words to songs Handel wrote in his musical Oratorio we now call *Handel's Messiah*, which is still performed each Christmas season all across the world.

Each of the names—Wonderful Counselor, Mighty God, Everlasting Father, and Prince of Peace—point to Jesus. Jesus is a prince with a wisdom that surpasses that of Solomon, and he brings a peace greater than that enjoyed during the reign of King David. Though it is obvious to us that this description points to Jesus, even Isaiah would have found it a mystery (Colossians 1:26). How could a child be both man and God? Who would this child of promise be and when would he be born?

Isaiah never saw the fulfillment of his words. Seven centuries would pass before Jesus was born. Now we get to look back and read God's fantastic promise with the full knowledge of the story of Christmas. With the coming of Christ and the revelation of the gospel, the mystery of the child hidden from Isaiah has been opened up for all to see. How it should fill us with wonder and cause us to sing, "Hallelujah! Hallelujah! And He shall reign forever and ever, King of kings and Lord of lords! Hallelujah! Hallelujah! Hallelujah! Hallelujah!" (Handel, "Hallelujah," from *Messiah*).

TALK ABOUT IT
Ask your family the following questions:

What names did Isaiah use to describe the child who would be born? *(Wonderful Counselor, Mighty God, Everlasting Father, Prince of Peace)*

Can you think of a way one of these names point to Jesus? *(Jesus was a wonderful counselor to all he met. He was able to heal the sick and rose from the dead with great power. Jesus compared himself to the Father [John 10:38] and promised us peace [John 14:27].)*

PRAY TOGETHER
Review the names Isaiah gave to Jesus and praise God for each one: Wonderful Counselor, Mighty God, Everlasting Father, Prince of Peace.

SING TOGETHER
(Sing the first song along with the CD or skip to the second song.)

He Who Is Mighty
Words and Music by Rebecca Elliott and Kate DeGraide.

VERSE 1
Oh, the mercy our God has shown
To those who sit in death's shadow
The sun on high pierced the night
Born was the Cornerstone
Unto us a Son is given, unto us a Child is born

VERSE 2
Oh, the freedom our Savior won
The yoke of sin has been broken
We once were slaves, bound in chains
Now, no condemnation
Unto us a Son is given, unto us a
Child is born

CHORUS

He Who is mighty has done a great thing
Taken on flesh, conquered death's sting
Shattered the darkness and lifted our shame
Holy is His name

BRIDGE

Now my soul magnifies the Lord
I rejoice in the God Who saves
I will trust His unfailing love
And sing His praises all my days

It Came upon the Midnight Clear

Words: Edmund H. Sears (1849). Music: CAROL, Richard S. Willis (1850).

VERSE 1

It came upon the midnight clear,
That glorious song of old,
From angels bending near the earth,
To touch their harps of gold:
"Peace on the earth, goodwill to men,
From heaven's all-gracious King."
The world in solemn stillness lay,
To hear the angels sing.

VERSE 2

Still through the cloven skies they come,
With peaceful wings unfurled,
And still their heavenly music floats
O'er all the weary world;
Above its sad and lowly plains,
They bend on hovering wing,
And ever o'er its Babel sounds
The blessèd angels sing.

VERSE 3

And ye, beneath life's crushing load,
Whose forms are bending low,
Who toil along the climbing way
With painful steps and slow,
Look now! for glad and golden hours
come swiftly on the wing.
O rest beside the weary road,
And hear the angels sing!

VERSE 4

For lo!, the days are hastening on,
By prophet bards foretold,
When with the ever-circling years
Comes round the age of gold
When peace shall over all the earth
Its ancient splendors fling,
And the whole world give back the song
Which now the angels sing.

FAMILY ACTIVITY
Color the Names

Have everyone pick one of the names in Isaiah's prophecy (Wonderful Counselor, Mighty God, Everlasting Father, Prince of Peace), draw it on their paper, and then color it or decorate the paper around it with a Christmas theme. Display the finished drawings.

The Angel's Announcement: A Visit to Mary

SUPPLIES NEEDED:

* one of your children's baby announcements or ultrasound photos
* freshly popped popcorn (air popped works best)
* fresh cranberries
* one large sharp sewing needle for each strand
* fishing monofilament or heavy-duty thread—one eight-foot length for each garland
* two large beads for each strand

WARM-UP

Your Own Baby Announcement

—Bring one of your own children's baby announcements or an ultrasound picture (if you've saved one) to family devotions. Tell a story of how you announced the birth of one of your children to family and friends.

READ THE BIBLE

Light the first Advent candle again and then read the Scripture below.

In the sixth month the angel Gabriel was sent from God to a city of Galilee named Nazareth, to a virgin betrothed to a man whose name was Joseph, of the house of David. And the virgin's name was Mary. And he came to her and said, "Greetings, O favored one, the Lord is with you!" But she was greatly troubled at the saying, and tried to discern what sort of greeting this might be. And the angel said to her, "Do not be afraid, Mary, for you have found favor with God. And behold, you will conceive in your womb and bear a son, and you shall call his name Jesus. He will be great and will be called the Son of the Most High. And the Lord God will give to him the throne of his father David, and he will reign over the house of Jacob forever, and of his kingdom there will be no end."

And Mary said to the angel, "How will this be, since I am a virgin?"

And the angel answered her, "The Holy Spirit will come upon you, and the power of the Most High will overshadow you; therefore the child to be born will be called holy—the Son of God. And behold, your relative Elizabeth in her old age has also conceived a son, and this is the sixth month with her who was called barren. For nothing will be impossible with God." And Mary said, "Behold, I am the servant of the Lord; let it be to me according to your word." And the angel departed from her. (Luke 1:26-38)

PICTURE IT

Do you remember the prophecy we learned earlier in the week? Isaiah said that a very special child was to be born to take the throne of the great King David. You can be sure that back in Isaiah's day people were excited about this special child. But after many years passed and no child came, the people's excitement faded. Isaiah's words, however, were not forgotten because God made sure they were recorded in the Bible.

Almost 700 years went by before the angel Gabriel came to Mary to announce the fulfillment of Isaiah's prophecy that a child would be born to the throne of David (Isaiah 9:7). Just before Isaiah told of the special child, he wrote that something wonderful would happen in Galilee (Isaiah 9:1). And wouldn't you know, that is exactly where

Mary was when Gabriel announced she would be the mother of the Son of God. Gabriel quoted from Isaiah saying that a child would be born: a son given to Mary. This child would reign on the throne of David forever and there would be no end to his kingdom. Something wonderful did happen in Galilee and Jesus grew up to be called the prophet from Galilee (Matthew 21:11).

TALK ABOUT IT

Mary trusted God's plan even though she didn't fully understand all of what he was doing. Talk together about a time when you have had to trust God's plan, even though you didn't understand what he was doing. *(We are all called to trust God through unexpected trials or difficulties and often find out after the fact how God used them to make us grow and mature.)*

PRAY TOGETHER

Read through the description of Jesus in Luke 1:32-33. Give thanks to God for each part of that description: that Jesus is the great Son of God, who reigns on the throne of David forever, and whose kingdom will have no end.

SING TOGETHER

(Sing along with the CD or a capella.)

What Child Is This

Words: William C. Dix (1865). Music: Greensleeves, 16th Century English melody.

VERSE 1

What Child is this who, laid to rest
On Mary's lap is sleeping?
Whom angels greet with anthems sweet
While shepherds watch are keeping?
This, this is Christ the King
Whom shepherds guard and angels sing
Haste, haste, to bring Him laud
The Babe, the Son of Mary

VERSE 2

Why lies He in such mean estate
Where ox and lamb are feeding?
Good Christians, fear, for sinners here
The silent Word is pleading
Nails, spear shall pierce Him through
The cross be borne for me, for you
Hail, hail the Word made flesh
The Babe, the Son of Mary

VERSE 3

So bring Him incense, gold and myrrh
Come peasant, king to own Him
The King of kings salvation brings
Let loving hearts enthrone Him

Raise, raise a song on high
The virgin sings her lullaby
Joy, joy for Christ is born
The Babe, the Son of Mary

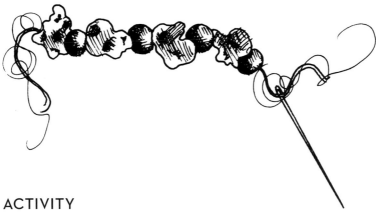

ACTIVITY
A Christmas Garland

Tie a bead to one end of each length of fishing monofilament or heavy-duty thread. Thread the popcorn and cranberries onto the monofilament or string. Come up with your own pattern. End with the second bead. Use the garland to decorate your tree, hang it in your bedroom or across the fireplace mantel.

Once you've finished decorating, go out after dark and enjoy your neighbors' Christmas decorations. Judge each display on a scale of one to ten. Pick the winner and consider bringing them some home-made cookies closer to Christmas. (You will make cookies as your last activity.)

The Fulfillment of God's Plan: Jesus Came in the Fullness of Time

SUPPLIES NEEDED:
* chocolate pudding

WARM-UP
Introduce the concept of the "fullness of time" by preparing a batch of chocolate pudding just before devotions and before the pudding has a chance to set. Explain to the children that you could eat (drink) the pudding now, or you could put it in the fridge until just the "fullness of time," to allow it to set and enjoy according to the plan on the box. Alternatively, set a timer for three minutes and place it on the table. Sit in silence as it counts down the minutes before you start reading the Scripture passage.

READ THE BIBLE
Light the first Advent candle again and then read the Scripture below.

I mean that the heir, as long as he is a child, is no different from a slave, though he is the owner of everything, but he is under guardians and managers until the date set by his father. In the same way we also, when we were children, were enslaved to the elementary principles of the world. But when the fullness of time had come, God sent forth his Son, born of woman, born under the law, to redeem those who were under the law, so that we might receive adoption as sons. And because you are sons, God has sent the Spirit of his Son into our hearts, crying,

"Abba! Father!" So you are no longer a slave, but a son, and if a son, then an heir through God. (Galatians 4:1-7)

PICTURE IT

The apostle Paul tells us that Gabriel's announcement to Mary was fulfilled, "when the fullness of time had come" (Galatians 4:4). The fullness of time is simply a way to say that Jesus came at just the right time. It took nearly 700 years for Isaiah's prophecy to finally be fulfilled. But God was not late and he wasn't early. Jesus came at just the right time—the fullness of time.

God planned for Jesus to come during a time when the Romans had brought peace to all the land. They conquered Europe, Asia, Palestine, and North Africa bringing in the "Pax Romana," the Roman Peace. This time of peace began before Jesus was born and lasted for more than a hundred years after his death and resurrection. This time of peace allowed the Romans to build a system of roads so that people could easily travel from country to country. They also made sure that everyone used a common language, Greek. It was on those roads, using the common language of the people, that the disciples of Jesus carried the gospel to the nations. God knew just what he was doing.

Gabriel's words to Mary came true. Mary became pregnant and gave birth, as did her cousin Elizabeth. Mary named her son Jesus; Elizabeth named her son John. When John grew up, God used him to announce Jesus as Messiah—as the "Lamb of God, who takes away the sin of the world" (John 1:29). When it was time for Jesus to start his ministry, he went to John to be baptized, not to repent of his own sin, but as our representative. Jesus insisted John baptize him to "fulfill all righteousness" (Matthew 3:15), and take our sins upon himself. Jesus's death on the cross provided a way for our sins to be forgiven and a way for all those who place their trust in Jesus to be adopted into the family of God.

TALK ABOUT IT

Do an Internet search on "ancient Roman roads" and show the images to your family. The Romans did such a good job building their roads that some of them have lasted 2,000 years and you can walk on them today!

Ask, "How do you think the Roman roads and the common language of Greek helped the spread of the gospel message?" *(Before Jesus ascended into heaven, he commanded his disciples to take the gospel to all nations. It was along the roads the Romans built that the early Christians traveled with the good news of Jesus Christ. The roads made the spread of the gospel quick and efficient. The common language made it easy for people to understand what the disciples were preaching.)*

PRAY TOGETHER

Thank God the Father for sending his son Jesus at the perfect time so that we might have our sins forgiven and be welcomed into the family of God.

SING TOGETHER

(Sing the first song along with the CD or skip to the second song.)

God Made Low

Words and Music by Jason Hansen and Bob Kauflin.

VERSE 1
Prophets promised long ago
A King would come to bring us hope
And now a virgin bears a son
The time to save the world has come

VERSE 2
Humble shepherds run in haste
To see the One the angels praised
In cattle stall they find a girl
Who holds the hope of all the world

VERSE 3
As He sleeps upon the hay
He holds the moon and stars in place

Though born an infant He remains
The sovereign God of endless days

VERSE 4
For all our sins one day He'll die
To make us sons of God on high
Let every heart prepare Him room
The promises have all come true

CHORUS
Emmanuel has come to us
The Christ is born, Hallelujah!
Our God made low to raise us up
Emmanuel, has come to us

Come Thou Long Expected Jesus

Words and Music by Charles Wesley, 1749.

VERSE 1

Come Thou long expected Jesus
Born to set Thy people free
From our fears and sins release us
Let us find our rest in Thee
Israel's strength and consolation
Hope of all the earth Thou art
Dear desire of every nation
Joy of every longing heart

VERSE 2

Born Thy people to deliver
Born a child and yet a King
Born to reign in us forever
Now Thy gracious kingdom bring
By Thine own eternal spirit
Rule in all our hearts alone
By Thine all sufficient merit
Raise us to Thy glorious throne

BARTIMAEUS: A CHRISTMAS STORY

CHAPTER ONE

Stop, Thief!

"Stop! Thief!" The shopkeeper shouted after the ragged boy who had slipped an apple into his pocket then turned and walked out the door without paying. At the sound of the man's voice, the boy took off through the ankle-deep snow, thin legs pumping.

Alerted by the shopkeeper's call, Sergeant O'Malley, a half a block away, caught a glimpse of a small dark figure moving against the white landscape. *He won't slip away from me this time,* the officer thought. He blew his whistle and took off after the boy. The lad was quick—much quicker than the officer—but the fresh tracks laid down in the new-fallen snow led directly to 1052 Marker Street. The footprints scaled a set of stairs and stopped at the dark, hand-carved chestnut door. A sign chiseled in the granite cornerstone read: Bartimaeus House, 1862.

The officer's face registered grim satisfaction as he followed the tracks up the stairs. He had been trying to catch the young thief for months. As he looked up at the familiar name on the door, the officer mused, "This might be the perfect place for him; I hope I can get him

to stay." The boy had all the earmarks of a recent orphan: he never stole anything of value, only what he needed to eat—a loaf of bread, a ring of baloney, an apple or two. The boy had always managed to stay a step or two ahead of Sergeant O'Malley. "But not today," he said as he turned the handle and opened the door.

Bartimaeus House got its start in 1852 when two-year-old Bartimaeus had been left on the doorstep of Jonathan Hawthorn's house. The little boy was one of hundreds of children similarly orphaned in New York, and the first of ten orphans Doc Hawthorn took into his home until they could be placed with adoptive families. When a heart attack claimed the doctor's life only a few years later, his wife used his estate to fund the construction of Bartimaeus House. More than fifty years had passed, but Bartimaeus House continued to care for orphans.

Frantically planning his escape, Christopher thought the old stone building looked like a school, and he reasoned he could hide unnoticed inside. It seemed like the perfect place to get lost in the crowd. Had he realized it was an orphanage, or that he was leaving such a clear trail in the fresh snow behind him, he would have kept running. To his surprise and relief, when he reached for the doorknob and turned it, the massive door swung open. He slipped inside and drew in a deep breath of the place. The warm room smelled like an old school. Christopher had been on his own since his parents died—his mother, last spring; his father, a year before that in the war. He shut his eyes and took in the sounds of a choir warming up in the distance. Their voices drew Christopher in and down a long, dim hallway.

As he drew closer to the open door near the end of the hall, he heard muffled voices and peeked around the corner of the open door. The singing started again: "Joy to the world, the Lord is come. Let earth receive her King . . ." Everyone was singing at his own tempo. *They sure need practice*, he thought as he stood undetected in the shadow of the doorway. About thirty children were in the chorus. An older girl was attempting to conduct, but no one was paying attention to her. Suddenly, the front door opened and closed with a thud. Christopher slipped into the room, plodding carefully in his oversized boots, and slid silently behind the faded drapes that framed the large windows now frosted with snow.

"But, Mary," a boy whined, "why do we have to sing Christmas songs when we can't even celebrate Christmas?"

The singing faltered then stopped altogether. "If Miss Roberts hears us stopping we'll have to practice even longer," Mary warned. "Besides, it's the only thing we do for Christmas. It's a tradition."

"So are candy canes and presents," the young boy shot back. "Why can't we really celebrate Christmas?"

A girl spoke up. "Miss Roberts says there is no use celebrating Christmas if you're not going to celebrate with a family."

"Miss Roberts says this, Miss Roberts says that," the boy whined in a sarcastic tone. "I don't care what Miss Roberts says or doesn't say."

A young girl on the front row said, "I'll bet there will be lots of folks going to the concert that could adopt us."

Mary shook her head. "Careful, Gwendolyn. Don't get your hopes up. Miss Roberts wouldn't approve. Remember, she was an orphan here when she was a child, and nobody ever adopted her. Besides, no one is adopting these days, not with the war going on." Mary walked over to the little girl, stroked her hair, and whispered, "I used to have your faith, but I gave up the hope of adoption long ago. It's time to move on, I suppose."

"Why aren't you practicing?" a voice challenged sharply, startling all but the few children who had seen her enter the room. Everyone snapped to attention and no one uttered a word as they looked at the woman who had just entered the room.

Christopher peeked out.

Mary said, "Miss Roberts, we—"

"Hush, Mary," Miss Roberts said. She stepped aside to let the policeman into the music room. "This is Sergeant O'Malley," she said. "Now where is he?"

The children looked at one another and shrugged.

"We know he's in here," O'Malley said.

"Where is who?" Mary asked, on behalf of the whole group.

"The thief!" O'Malley blurted out. "That's who."

"Thief?" Mary gasped.

"Officer O'Malley followed a young boy—a thief!—in through our front door," Miss Roberts explained. "Wet melting snow tracks led down the hallway from the front door right to this . . . puddle of water." She looked down at a circle of water just on the threshold.

"So, out with it," O'Malley commanded. "Where is he?"

Christopher held his breath and did his best to stand absolutely still. *One ripple of the drapes and he was a goner!*

Every eye fixed on the water still pooled at the doorway but no one had an answer. They simply looked at each other.

"Well, then," Sergeant O'Malley said, "we'll just use some good old fashioned detective work . . . Let's follow these three small drops of water that lead from this telltale puddle in the doorway over here . . . to the left side of the room."

Just before the officer reached him, Christopher shot out from behind the drapes and bolted toward the door. Dodging the officer, he

slammed straight into Miss Roberts, who held him securely by his collar.

"Let me go!" he shouted, struggling to break free. But it was no use. A second later, the officer had grabbed him.

"What's your name?" the sergeant asked him.

"Christopher," he spat.

"Christopher who?" the sergeant continued.

Christopher blinked several times but said nothing.

O'Malley rubbed his chin thoughtfully. "The choice is simple, Christopher. You can either stay here at Bartimaeus or head straight to the judge. The choice is yours, but if you go to the judge you'll be facing a long list of charges," he warned. "You've been stealing from the market for months now. The judge will most likely turn you over to the Children's Aid Society, and they'll ship you out on one of their orphan trains."

The officer was right. Rumors ran wild on the street about the orphan trains that hauled children off to faraway placed to be peddled for their farm labor. If he didn't agree to stay, Christopher would be on his way out west to some farm in the middle of nowhere to work long days and spend his nights in a cold basement crawling with critters while the farmer's own children were safe and sound in their warm beds. At least Bartimaeus was warm. "I'll stay," he said. *Stay for a few months, that is, until the weather turns warmer. Then I can skip out and be back on the run.*

O'Malley, who seemed to be reading his mind, said, "'Don't you even think of leaving, you hear?" He wagged his finger an inch from Christopher's nose to punctuate his stern words. "One bad report, just one . . . or if I ever so much as catch you outside again, it's the slammer for you, young man. You shook us for months in the warm weather, but you'll die out there in the cold." Sleet was now clicking against the panes.

"I said I'll stay," Christopher repeated. Truth was, he had never been alone at Christmastime, and he surely didn't like the cold, much less the snow.

The sergeant tipped his hat and said, "Well, I guess that will do it for now. Thank you, Miss Roberts." He bid her a good day, hitched up his pants by the belt heavy with the instruments of his law-keeping trade, then turned sharply, clicked his heels with military precision, and strode out of the room.

After a half-second pause to catch her breath, Miss Roberts addressed the children. "Jake, you will show Christopher to the washbasin and help him get properly clean for dinner. Find him some trousers and a shirt from the boy's box in the spare room. The rest of you, wash your hands at once and report to the dining room. I am heading over to the YMCA to talk to the new director about our performance. Oh, and Christopher, welcome to Bartimaeus. You'll have the same privileges as the other children: warm meals, warm clothes, and a warm home. But let this be fair warning to you: You mess up, you lose them all. Do you understand?"

"Yes," Christopher said, nodding.

"Very well, then." She looked at the rest of the children. "Don't forget your studies after dinner. Bedtime is 9:30." She pointed to the clock. Then she turned and exited the room, her hard-soled shoes thumping down the hallway. The children stood motionless and listened for the loud clap of the door closing behind her.

God's Promise: The Greatest Proof of All

SUPPLIES NEEDED:

* ✷ driver's license
* ✷ white paper
* ✷ colored pencils and crayons
* ✷ gift box and gift wrap and bow
* ✷ gift of your choice

WARM-UP

Prove It to Me

—Show your driver's license to your family. Ask your children this question: How can I prove to someone that I am really _____ (insert your name). Let's say a valuable package came to the post office and I went there to pick it up. How could I prove to the clerk it was really me and not someone else? (The answer of course is that you could pull out your identification to prove you are who you say you are.) Pass your driver's license around and allow your children to see it.

—Next ask your children how God proves that he is who he says that he is. He doesn't have a driver's license to pull out and show. *(God proves he is who he says he is by the things that he does. For example, God made the stars and they are so amazing that they testify to his glorious power. When God sent Moses to speak to Pharaoh, he told him to throw down his staff and it would become a snake. God said he would use this sign to prove he was God and that he had authority to command Pharoah.)*

—Today we are going to learn about a very special sign God gave to prove something to a King named Ahaz.

READ THE BIBLE

Light the first and second Advent candles and then read the Scripture below.

Again the Lord spoke to Ahaz, "Ask a sign of the LORD your God; let it be deep as Sheol or high as heaven." But Ahaz said, "I will not ask, and I will not put the LORD to the test." And [Isaiah] said, "Hear then, O house of David! Is it too little for you to weary men, that you weary my God also? Therefore the LORD himself will give you a sign. Behold, the virgin shall conceive and bear a son, and shall call his name Immanuel." (Isaiah 7:10-14)

PICTURE IT

King Ahaz was in trouble: an enemy army bearing down, ready to attack his country. God sent the prophet Isaiah to Ahaz to calm his fears. Isaiah told Ahaz not to worry; God would protect him. To prove himself powerful enough to protect Ahaz, God told him to ask for a sign, for some proof. It could be anything as high as the stars. Imagine Ahaz saying to God, "If it is really true then spell my name with stars in the sky." God would have spelled his name with stars.

Ahaz was afraid to ask God for a sign, he thought it was disrespectful. But God wanted to give Ahaz a sign. So God spoke through Isaiah and gave Ahaz the greatest sign that has ever been given: "the virgin shall conceive and bear a son, and shall call his name Immanuel," which means, "God with us." Imagine that, a woman who knew no man, would give birth to a son, but not just any son, this special child would be God himself come down from heaven to earth, born as a baby.

While God did protect Ahaz from his enemies, Ahaz had no idea what the sign Isaiah brought to him meant. But today, looking back, we know that the virgin Isaiah spoke of was Mary and her Son was Jesus, Immanuel, God with us. Today we understand that God was giving a sign so that we could all believe God is who he says he is. Jesus proved that he was God, when, after dying on the cross, he rose again from the dead, just as he said.

TALK ABOUT IT

Show your family the baby Jesus figure from your manger set. Ask if they can remember the special name God gave Jesus before he was born that tells us he was God. *(The name is Immanuel.)*

Then ask, "What does the name Immanuel mean and why was the sign God gave Ahaz the greatest sign of all? *(Immanuel means "God with us." God's word to Ahaz that he would send his son as a baby to earth is the greatest sign of God's saving love. More than saving Ahaz from attack, God's word to Ahaz pointed to a day when God would save us all through Jesus who grew up to die on the cross for our sins.)*

PRAY TOGETHER

Thank God for sending us his only Son, Jesus, to live a perfect life for us and die on the cross to take our sins away.

SING TOGETHER

(Sing along with the CD or a capella.)

O Come, O Come Emmanuel

Original words (vv. 1–2) by an unknown author, translated by John M. Neale (1851). Alt. and add. words (vv. 3–5) by Steve Cook and Bob Kauflin. Music: Veni Emmanuel, arranged by Thomas Helmore (1856).

VERSE 1
O come, O come, Emmanuel
And ransom captive Israel
That mourns in lonely exile here
Until the Son of God appear
Rejoice! Rejoice! Emmanuel
Shall come to thee, O Israel!

VERSE 2
O come, Thou Dayspring from on high
And cause Thy light on us to rise
Disperse the gloomy clouds of night

And death's dark shadow put to flight
Rejoice! Rejoice! Emmanuel
Shall come to thee, O Israel!

VERSE 3
O come, O come, true prophet of the LORD
And turn the key to heaven's door
Be Thou our comforter and guide
And lead us to the Father's side
Rejoice! Rejoice! Emmanuel
Shall by His word our darkness dispel

VERSE 4	VERSE 5
O come, our Great High Priest, and intercede	O Come, Thou King of nations bring
Thy sacrifice our only plea	An end to all our suffering
The judgment we no longer fear	Bid every pain and sorrow cease
Thy precious blood has brought us near	And reign now as our Prince of Peace
Rejoice! Rejoice! Emmanuel	Rejoice! Rejoice! Emmanuel
Has banished every fear of hell	Shall come again with us to dwell

ACTIVITY
A Christmas Gift

Christmas presents a wonderful opportunity to give a gift to someone in need. Think of a person or family you know that you don't normally exchange gifts with but who is in need this Christmas season. Once you've identified the person or family, consider what gift would bless them.

Read John 3:16, "For God so loved the world, that he gave his only Son, that whoever believes in him should not perish but have eternal life." Remember that Jesus Christ was a precious gift to all of us from God the Father. Use God's generosity toward us to motivate you to be generous to another person or family in need. Then discuss as a family what gift you should give to them.

Purchase or make and wrap the gift. Make a card with the paper and colored pencils and crayons. Have each person in your family sign the card and then go together to deliver your gift. On your way home, thank God again for the gift of his Son, Jesus Christ, and for the joy of giving, which allows us to imitate God's kindness toward us.

The Angel's Announcement: Joseph's Dream

WARM-UP

Can You Remember a Dream?

We all have dreams, but it is a really special event for God to send an angel with a message. Most of the time we forget our dreams, but sometimes we remember. Can you remember a dream you had? Take time as a family to share a dream each person remembers, then talk about how unusual Joseph's dream must have been.

READ THE BIBLE

Light the first and second Advent candles again and then read the Scripture below.

> *Now the birth of Jesus Christ took place in this way. When his mother Mary had been betrothed to Joseph, before they came together she was found to be with child from the Holy Spirit. And her husband Joseph, being a just man and unwilling to put her to shame, resolved to divorce her quietly. But as he considered these things, behold, an angel of the Lord appeared to him in a dream, saying, "Joseph, son of David, do not fear to take Mary as your wife, for that which is conceived in her is from the Holy Spirit. She will bear a son, and you shall call his name Jesus, for he will save his people from their sins." All this took place to fulfill what the Lord had spoken by the prophet: "Behold, the virgin shall conceive and bear a son, and they shall call his name Immanuel" (which means, God with us).*

When Joseph woke from sleep, he did as the angel of the Lord commanded him: he took his wife, but knew her not until she had given birth to a son. And he called his name Jesus. (Matthew 1:18-25)

PICTURE IT

Joseph loved Mary: they were engaged to be married. But Joseph's excitement for their wedding was crushed when he found out that Mary was going to have a baby by someone else! According to law and custom, Joseph was expected to break his engagement to (divorce) Mary, and send her away. But rather than make a big deal out of the situation, Joseph decided he would send her away quietly, so fewer people would know. Mary surely had told Joseph the story of the angel's visit, but you can imagine how hard it was for Joseph to believe.

But before Joseph broke off the engagement, an angel paid him a visit as well, this time in a dream. The angel of the Lord, who appeared to Joseph, announced to him a part of Isaiah's prophecy, which confirmed Mary's story. Now he knew Mary was telling him the truth. What a flood of joy must have poured over Joseph's heart as he realized he didn't have to send Mary away. Imagine Mary's excitement when Joseph told her of his dream and then embraced her. Mary wouldn't have to do this alone. Joseph adopted the child as his own, and in obedience to the angel, named his son Jesus.

TALK ABOUT IT

Discuss why it was important for the angel to quote the Bible when he spoke to Joseph in his dream. *(Joseph was a godly man who knew the Scriptures. When the angel quoted the prophet Isaiah 7:14, Joseph was reminded of the promise that God was going to give a baby to a woman who wasn't married yet and the baby would be Immanuel, God with us. That helped Joseph to understand Mary's story about the angel's visit to her. Open up your Bible to Isaiah 7:14 and allow the children to see the quote for themselves.)*

PRAY TOGETHER

Thank God for his amazing plan to send his Son Jesus into the world. Thank God for giving Joseph the courage to marry Mary and adopt Jesus as his own son.

SING TOGETHER

(Sing the first song along with the CD or skip to the second song.)

One Still Night

Words and Music by Neil and Kate DeGraide.

VERSE 1
One still night, Mary awoke
Stirred by an angel, she trembled as he spoke
One small child, would soon be born
The King of kings will wear a crown of thorns

VERSE 2
One still night, while Joseph dreamed
He saw a vision within his troubled sleep
One small child, his bride would give
Deliverer delivered, to save us from our sin

BRIDGE
And to His kingdom there'll be no end

And the government shall be on His shoulders
Immanuel

VERSE 3
One still night, a light was shown
That all the darkness could never overcome

CHORUS
"Glory to God," the angels sang
"Immanuel was born for you this day
Peace on earth, good will toward men
Immanuel has come to Bethlehem
Immanuel has come to Bethlehem"

Away in a Manger

First two stanzas attributed to unknown author; third stanza written by John McFarland (1904).

VERSE 1
Away in a manger,
no crib for a bed,
The little Lord Jesus laid down His sweet head.
The stars in the sky looked down where He lay,
The little Lord Jesus asleep on the hay.

VERSE 2
The cattle are lowing,
the baby awakes,
But little Lord Jesus no crying He makes.

I love Thee, Lord Jesus,
look down from the sky
And stay by my cradle till morning is nigh.

VERSE 3
Be near me, Lord Jesus,
I ask Thee to stay
Close by me forever,
and love me, I pray.
Bless all the dear children in thy tender care,
And fit us for heaven, to live with Thee there.

The Fulfillment of God's Plan: The Word Became Flesh

SUPPLIES NEEDED:
* 8 1/2" x 11" sheet of paper

WARM-UP
Three Names for Jesus

Fold a standard piece of paper lengthwise into thirds. In each of the parts write one of the following: Jesus, The Word, and Immanuel. Tape the edges of the paper together to form a triangular nameplate-like. Use the nameplate to help your children understand that all three names describe the Son of God. The Word is the name John gives God's Son and tells us that he has always lived with the Father. Immanuel is the name Isaiah used to describe the Word coming down to earth. Jesus is the name the angel told Joseph to give his son, born in Bethlehem.

READ THE BIBLE
Light the first and second Advent candles again and then read the Scripture below.

> *In the beginning was the Word, and the Word was with God, and the Word was God. He was in the beginning with God. All things were made through him, and without him was not any thing made that was made. In him was life, and the life was the light of men. The light shines in the darkness, and the darkness*

has not overcome it. . . . And the Word became flesh and dwelt among us, and we have seen his glory, glory as of the only Son from the Father, full of grace and truth. (John 1:1-5, 14)

PICTURE IT

Matthew and Luke's gospels begin with the story of the birth of Jesus in Bethlehem, but John tells the story a very different way. He describes Jesus as the Word of God. Did you ever think of Jesus as the Word of God who always lived and never had a beginning? When we think of Jesus, the Son of God, we think of his birth in a stable. But that is not really his beginning. Before Jesus was born, the eternal Son of God, whom John calls the Word of God, lived with his Father in heaven. Then, when the time was just right, God sent his Son into the world as a baby. The Word of God became flesh and dwelt, or lived, with us here on earth as the child of Mary and Joseph. Jesus was more than a man; Jesus was God who came to earth to live among us. Jesus was Immanuel—God with us.

The apostle John wanted us to be sure that we understood that Jesus was God. John says that Jesus existed from the beginning as God, and that he created the world and all that we see. Then God the Son, the living Word, came down to earth to live among men. John saw Jesus do things that only God could do. John saw Jesus heal the sick, multiply the fishes and the loaves, and be transformed into glorious splendor at the transfiguration (Matthew 17:1-2). John watched Jesus die upon the cross (John 19:26-27), and saw him raised again from the dead (John 20:19). Finally John saw Jesus ascend into the sky and go back to God the Father in heaven (Acts 1:9). John wanted to make sure we knew that Jesus was more than a baby in a manger. The words of the angel were fulfilled—Jesus really was our Immanuel, God with us.

TALK ABOUT IT

Ask, "Why is Immanuel such a good name for Jesus?" *(First, help your children remember what the name Immanuel means—God with us.*

Then draw from the passage in John, who said that all things were made through Jesus and that he is God! There is no better name to describe God coming down as a man to be with us than Immanuel— God with us.)

PRAY TOGETHER
Thank the Lord in prayer for sending Jesus as our Immanuel.

SING TOGETHER
(Sing the first song along with the CD or skip to the second song.)

Before the Skies
Original words by Isaac Watts. Alternate words and music by Doug Plank.

VERSE 1
Before the skies were stretched abroad
From everlasting was the Word
God was He; the Word was God
And He must be adored

VERSE 2
By the Word all came to be
The universe and all contained
Showing God's authority
His power and His reign

REFRAIN:
Glory, glory, glory in the highest
Glory, glory, glory God is with us, with us

VERSE 3
Though His glories still proceed

Never changing from our Lord
He laid down His majesty
And took on human form

VERSE 4
Mortals here beheld His face
The Heav'nly Father's perfect Son
Full of truth and full of grace
The Savior now has come!

VERSE 5
He gave up His life in love
So our lips could gladly tell
Christ, the Word, has come to us
Our Lord, Immanuel

Silent Night

Written by Franz Xaver Gruber and Josef Mohr, best known in the English translation by John Freeman Young.

VERSE 1

Silent night, holy night!
All is calm, All is bright
Round yon Virgin, Mother and Child
Holy Infant so Tender and mild,
Sleep in heavenly peace,
Sleep in heavenly peace.

VERSE 2

Silent night, holy night!
Shepherds quake at the sight!
Glories stream from heaven afar;

Heavenly hosts sing Al-le-lu-ia!
Christ the Savior is born!
Christ the Savior is born!

VERSE 3

Silent night! Holy night!
Son of God love's pure light
Radiant beams from thy holy face
With the dawn of redeeming grace,
Jesus, Lord at thy birth,
Jesus, Lord at thy birth.

BARTIMAEUS: A CHRISTMAS STORY

CHAPTER TWO

It's a Grueling Life

The moment the door slammed shut signaling Miss Roberts's exit, one of the boys shouted, "Last one to dinner has to wash the dishes!" All at once the thirty or so children took off like a flock of spooked geese lifting off a pond. A narrow door at the back of the room slowed the stampede and funneled them one by one into a short hallway and into the washrooms where the crowd split—girls to the left, boys to the right. Two lines formed behind the sinks in the boys' washroom. Soap, soap-rub, rub-rinse, rinse-dry, dry: their hand washing routine resembled linework in a manufacturing plant. They put in as little effort as possible to pass the hand check, so as to keep their position in the race to dinner.

"Hey, what about my new clothes?" Christopher asked Jake, who was shaking the excess water from his hands.

"Plenty of time for playing dress-up after we eat. I'm not getting stuck doing dishes for your new clothes." Jake took off and pushed through the door with Christopher close behind. They passed a few

of the others before sliding to a halt to avoid crashing into the line stopped at the back of the dining room.

I didn't do too bad, considering I had no idea where to go, Christopher thought. He was fifth from last in line. The last four in line did the dishes, he was told. "That is, unless your hands aren't clean enough," Jake said. "In that case you go to the back of the line." Christopher looked down at his hands, still red and damp from washing. He gave them an extra rub, drying them on his shirt. They seemed clean enough.

He had always hated washing for dinner, but six months on the street has a way of changing the way a fellow looks at things. The hot water had felt good on his hands and it had been a long time since he had a home-cooked meal. As he stood in line he dreamed of roast beef and mashed potatoes. He was too far back in line to see through the serving window and the line hadn't started moving yet. The dining room was almost as large as the music room where they had been singing. It was filled with heavy oak tables and benches with enough seats for 100 or more children. Dark wood panels and trim lined the walls and the plastered ceiling was painted with an interesting design. The line of hungry children snaked around the room, turned the first corner, and stopped just short of the kitchen.

A moment later, a door opened at the back of the kitchen and a woman with a sturdy frame and warm smile walked through it.

Jake said, "That's Mrs. Schultz, the cook."

The woman stepped up to the window and leaned over the counter said, "Good evening, children." Then after a quick scan of the line, she continued. "Glad to see you, Christopher. Welcome to Bartimaeus. We don't have much to spare with the war going on and all. But what we have will fill and warm your belly. There's plenty of porridge to go round," she said, shaking a shallow ladle, "and I've salted it just right, you know. Now then, Bobby, will you give thanks?"

Bobby gave a wink to the cook then made quick work of the prayer and immediately the line began to move. "So, what were you guessing we would be having for dinner—roast beef, roast chicken, or roast pork?" asked a girl standing next to Christopher. "It's OK," she said. "My name is Alice." She extended her hand. "We all come in hoping for something good," she said. "I was hoping for roast pork myself. Come on, you didn't expect *gruel* for dinner. The cook calls it 'porridge,' but we call it *gruel*. Well?"

"Well what?" Christopher said as he struggled with the idea of eating porridge for dinner. He was sure he smelled roast beef wafting through the hallway earlier. Perhaps they would have a real meal on Sunday. His family always had a special meal on Sunday.

"Well, what were you hoping we'd have?" she persisted.

"Beef," he said with a shy nod. "I was dreaming of roast beef and potatoes."

Then Alice turned to the crowd and shouted: "Hear that, boys? Christopher here was hoping for roast beef. Roast beef is now tied at nine with roast chicken for the lead over pork."

"Do you eat porridge every day for dinner? What's for lunch and breakfast?" he asked, all at once.

"It's gruel, my friend," Alice said. "Gruel, gruel, gruel: breakfast, lunch, and dinner."

"*Every* meal?" Christopher asked incredulously.

"OK!" the cook said, winking now at Alice, and shouting loudly enough to catch all their attention. "Does anyone have a new verse for me?"

"I've got a new one," Timothy said.

"Oh you do, eh?" the cook said, smiling. "Let me hear it, then."

Without further introduction, one of the boys snapped his fingers, hummed a note to the beat, and the children all started to sing:

"It's a grueling life, a grueling life
Here at Bart-a-maeus
Eat gruel every morn, eat gruel every night
That is what they like to feed us
I've lived here far as I remember
I haven't lived anywhere else.
Except for one day in November,
When a turkey is pulled off the shelf
We. Eat. Gruel."

Then a boy named Timmy jumped up on a bench and started to sing a solo:

"It's not so bad after a month or so
There are actually good days and bad
The cook some days salts it just right, ya know
Oh the best gruel that you'll ever have
So. Eat. Gruel."

The children applauded, clapping and whooping, and led back to the chorus singing louder than ever. Even the cook joined in, which puzzled Christopher as they were really complaining about her meal. After the second chorus ended, others took turns with verses, each followed by the chorus again. Six of the boys in front of Christopher grabbed their bowls, spoons, and tin cups off the serving line and formed a percussion section and kept on laying down a beat until it was their turn in line, all singing in perfect harmony.

I can't believe these are the same kids, Christopher thought, remembering how they had sung that awful version of "Joy to the World" earlier. The song continued till the last person had made it through the line. Then, with steaming hot bowls all lined up on the tables, a double chorus finished the song. The cook broke out in loud clapping and lavished compliments on them all. She smiled broadly, and it was clear that she really loved all the children at Bartimaeus.

Suddenly Christopher looked down at the warm bowl, cupped in his hands. He was so caught up with the song that he didn't even notice what the cook dropped in his bowl, a generous portion of hearty beef stew with carrots and potatoes! "This isn't porridge," he shouted, "this is beef stew!"

The room grew quiet then erupted in laughter.

"Welcome to Bartimaeus," Mrs. Schultz said with a smile, then turned to the children. "We fooled another one, kids." The children cheered. They loved Mrs. Shultz and sang the gruel song every night at dinnertime when Miss Roberts was out of earshot. So far, they never got caught and had at least a dozen verses written.

Things quieted down as the children eagerly downed their stew. In a minute the murmur began in earnest and rose to a dull roar with everyone eagerly chatting about the day's events. The children were free to talk at meals, and with Miss Roberts away, they had little restraint. The cook continued dancing and humming the melody of their song while those assigned to kitchen duty collected the empty bowls from the tables and carried them through a side door to the kitchen sink.

Christopher leaned over and asked one of the older boys, "Why don't you have decorations up for Christmas?"

"Look around, buddy," the boy told him, looking up from his bowl. "This is reality. It's a tough world out there. Nobody cares. Nobody wants us. Why pretend anything different?"

"You should know that," Timothy added. "Having to steal food to survive. It's all a bunch of hype. Who wants Christmas anyway? Most of us here have never even had Christmas. What's to miss about it?"

"It's not only the decorations," Christopher answered. "There's something special about it. Every Christmas," Christopher said, remembering, "my dad would put up the tree, and then we would string popcorn and cranberry garlands. When the tree was all decorated, we'd set out the manger—all but the baby Jesus. We'd put the shepherds off to the left; the wise men off to the right."

When he looked up Christopher realized that the whole room was quiet and everyone was listening to him. He thought about what Timothy had said . . . "Most of us here have never even had Christmas." Christopher realized that he wasn't your average Bartimaeus orphan; he used to have a family. He looked around and could tell that most of these children had never had a family and had no family memories. That's why his story captured their attention so. Even the cook was listening in.

"Why were the shepherds and wise men off to the side?" one of the little girls asked.

"Why, they don't come to visit until the baby is born," Christopher said, turning his head in her direction. "On Christmas Eve, the last thing before I went to bed, my mom would hand me a little hand-carved wooden chest. It was like a treasure." He paused and made a gesture as if to take the chest into his hands. "You had to hold it carefully and do it just right." As the children listened, captivated by the story of his family at Christmas, Christopher rose from the table and dramatized his Christmas past like an act from a play.

"Very carefully I'd pop open the clasp and open the box. I'd lightly brush aside the cotton to reveal a little porcelain baby packed safely in a bed of white. Then, I carried it over to our tree and bent down." Christopher was on his knees kneeling before an imaginary tree. "Then, while I placed the baby in the tiny manger, my mom—"Christopher paused for a moment and felt a tear slither down his cheek. "Mom moved the shepherds close together, and then Dad moved the wise men. We would sing 'Joy to the World.'" Christopher paused, quietly caught up in the sweet memory.

"Not that song again," Timothy interrupted. "We have to sing that song every year." The other children were quick to join him in voicing their displeasure. Suddenly everyone was quiet, as Miss Roberts and a tall man they had never met before entered the room.

The tall man stepped forward toward the children and cleared his throat. "Perhaps I ought to introduce myself," he said in a booming voice that echoed in the large dining hall. "My name is Colonel Jackson, but folks just call me Colonel. I'm just back from my second tour in the army, in a season of reconditioning." The Colonel nodded down toward his leg and the children noticed he was leaning on a cane. I'm taking over management of the YMCA for a while. The director, in a manner of speaking, has taken my place, called upon to serve our country. I offered to step into his role during my rehabilitation. Now, your guardian here," he said, pointing to Miss Roberts, "tells me you're nowhere near ready to perform in our Christmas program this year."

Miss Roberts spoke up. "So you will excuse us from the program, sir? It is so hard on the children, singing in front of families when there is little hope they will ever be adopted themselves."

Ignoring her comments, the Colonel addressed the children as he paced in front of them, stopping occasionally to point his cane. "I'm not ready to retreat. I just came from the trenches, you know. I am used to impossible odds. Saw young boys turned into men." The Colonel looked at the children thoughtfully and then turned to Miss Roberts. "Perhaps I could have some time with the children tomorrow morning. We don't have much time before the program. Perhaps a little pep talk and practice might help?" The Colonel smiled and winked at Miss Roberts.

"Looks like we're doomed to sing that sorry old song again," one of the children whispered to the others.

"You are welcome to come at 10:00," Miss Roberts replied. "If you desire, the children can move their practice session to the morning and if you don't mind, I'll use the time to catch up on a bit of paperwork."

"Very well, then," the Colonel replied. "I'll be back in the morning. Good day, children." Then he turned and walked out the door.

God's Promise: It Will Happen in Bethlehem

SUPPLIES NEEDED:

* church invitations *(If your church doesn't have invitations to use for Christmas, have your children draw a Christmas scene on a sheet of paper and write the Christmas service times for your church and your church address on the bottom. Photocopy the invitation to pass out as you carol, to invite your neighbors and friends to join you for church this Christmas season.)*

WARM-UP

A Little More about the Town

At Christmas time, we often sing "O Little Town of Bethlehem," but do you know anything about that famous Christmas town? Do an Internet search on the ancient city of Bethlehem and show your family a few photos of the city. Then relate the following facts about Bethlehem:

—Jacob's wife, Rachel, is buried there and you can still visit the grave site today (Genesis 35:19-20).

—It was the birthplace of King David—the same person who killed the giant Goliath (1 Samuel 16:18-20).

—Bethlehem is about five miles south of the city of Jerusalem.

—Today, Bethlehem has a large Christian population.

READ THE BIBLE

Light the first, second, and third Advent candles and then read the Scripture below.

Now muster your troops, O daughter of troops; siege is laid against us; with a rod they strike the judge of Israel on the cheek. But you, O Bethlehem Ephrathah, who are too little to be among the clans of Judah, from you shall come forth for me one who is to be ruler in Israel, whose coming forth is from of old, from ancient days. (Micah 5:1-2)

PICTURE IT

A boy named David was born in the district of Ephrathah (1 Samuel 17:12) in Bethlehem and grew up tending his father Jesse's sheep. When the time came for Samuel to anoint a new king over Israel, God sent him to Jesse's house to anoint one of his sons. David, considered too young and insignificant to be anointed king, remained out in the fields tending the sheep. He was, however, God's choice, for God told Samuel that man looks at the outer appearance but God looks at the heart. So Samuel passed over the older, stronger brothers and sent for David and anointed him King of Israel (1 Samuel 16:13). David became the greatest king that ever ruled over Israel, and Bethlehem became known as the City of David because this famous king was born there.

Long after David's reign as king of Israel, the prophet Micah foretold that God would again choose a king from Bethlehem, in the land of Ephrathah. But it would take hundreds of years more before God fulfilled that prophetic word with the birth of Jesus. In that day wise men from the East followed a star in search of the newborn king of the Jews. When they came to Jerusalem, they asked King Herod if he knew where to find the newborn king. Herod had no idea where the baby was and was very jealous. He called for the scribes and chief priests and asked them if they knew. The religious rulers directed his attention to Micah's prophecy, which pointed to Bethlehem. Once again a ruler would come from this insignificant town and once again God's choice involved the most unlikely beginning—a baby, born in a stable.

TALK ABOUT IT

Ask, "In the story, what happened after Herod sent the wise men on their way to Bethlehem?" *(Herod, secretly planning to kill the child, asked the wise men to tell him the location of the child. In a dream, God warned them about Herod's plan, so they never sent back word and traveled a different way home [see Matthew 2:1-14].)*

PRAY TOGETHER

Praise God for the birth of Jesus, our humble King, born in a stable. Thank God for protecting Jesus against Herod's evil plan.

SING TOGETHER

(Sing the first song along with the CD or skip to the second song.)

Who Would Have Dreamed

Words and Music by Jason Hansen and Bob Kauflin

VERSE 1

On a starlit hillside, shepherds watched their sheep
Slowly, David's city drifted off to sleep
But to this little town of no great renown
The Lord had a promise to keep

VERSE 2

Prophets had foretold it, a mighty King would come
Long-awaited Ruler, God's anointed one
But the Sovereign of all looked helpless and small
As God gave the world His own Son

CHORUS

And who would have dreamed or ever foreseen
That we could hold God in our hands?
The Giver of Life is born in the night
Revealing God's glorious plan
To save the world

VERSE 3

Wondrous gift of heaven: the Father sends the Son
Planned from time eternal, moved by holy love
He will carry our curse and death He'll reverse
So we can be daughters and sons

O Little Town of Bethlehem

Words: Phillips Brooks, 1867. Music: St. Louis, Lewis H. Redner, 1868.

VERSE 1

O little town of Bethlehem,
How still we see thee lie!
Above thy deep and dreamless sleep
The silent stars go by;
Yet in thy dark streets shineth
The everlasting Light;
The hopes and fears of all the years
Are met in thee to-night.

VERSE 2

For Christ is born of Mary,
And, gathered all above,
While mortals sleep,
the angels keep
Their watch of wondering love.

O morning stars, together
Proclaim the holy birth!
And praises sing to God the King,
And peace to men on earth.

VERSE 3

O holy Child of Bethlehem!
Descend to us, we pray;
Cast out our sin,
and enter in,
Be born in us to-day.
We hear the Christmas angels
The great glad tidings tell;
Oh, come to us, abide with us,
Our Lord Emmanuel!

ACTIVITY
Caroling Together

Visit your neighbors and invite those who may not have a church home to your Christmas services. Folks who don't attend church regularly will often enjoy attending church at Christmas.

The Angel's Announcement: A Visit to the Shepherds

SUPPLIES NEEDED:
* manger scene

WARM-UP
Set up a Manger Scene

Now that we've come to the place in our devotions where Jesus is born, set up a manger scene in your home.

READ THE BIBLE
Light the first, second, and third Advent candles again and then read the Scripture.

And in the same region there were shepherds out in the field, keeping watch over their flock by night. And an angel of the Lord appeared to them, and the glory of the Lord shone around them, and they were filled with great fear. And the angel said to them, "Fear not, for behold, I bring you good news of great joy that will be for all the people. For unto you is born this day in the city of David a Savior, who is Christ the Lord. And this will be a sign for you: you will find a baby wrapped in swaddling cloths and lying in a manger." And suddenly there was with the angel a multitude of the heavenly host praising God and saying, "Glory to God in the highest, and on earth peace among those with whom he is pleased!"

When the angels went away from them into heaven, the shepherds said to one another, "Let us go over to Bethlehem and see this thing that has happened, which the Lord has made known to us." And they went with haste and found Mary and Joseph, and the baby lying in a manger. And when they saw it, they made known the saying that had been told them concerning this child. And all who heard it wondered at what the shepherds told them. But Mary treasured up all these things, pondering them in her heart. And the shepherds returned, glorifying and praising God for all they had heard and seen, as it had been told them. (Luke 2:8-20)

THINK ABOUT IT

Imagine the shepherds, tired from the day's work of guiding their sheep from pasture to pasture, now gathered together to take turns on the night watch against wolves and robbers. Suddenly a blinding light pierces the darkness of night and an angel appears. They cower in fear as their eyes fail to adjust to the burst of light. The angel of the Lord tries to calm their fear, then announces the birth of the Christ child in the city of David, the very place Micah said it would take place. After telling the shepherds how to find the baby Jesus, the night sky exploded with angels bursting into song.

The shepherds were so affected by the message that they left their sheep, something shepherds just don't do. When they arrived in Bethlehem, they found Jesus just as the angel said, lying in a manger. They report the angels' visit to Mary who treasures their words in her heart. Mary wasn't surprised by their story of angels. After all, she had had her own encounter with the angel Gabriel, not to mention Joseph's dream. Mary sat there, looking down at the baby Jesus, wondering how all these things fit together in God's plan.

TALK ABOUT IT

Ask, "Why do you think God had his son born in a stable rather than a palace?" *(Luke tells us that the reason Jesus was born in a stable is that there was no room for him in the inn. The real reason was to show all of us the humility of Jesus. Look up Philippians 2:6-7.)*

PRAY TOGETHER

Thank Jesus for giving up his heavenly throne to come into a sinful world to save us from our sins.

SING TOGETHER

(Sing along with the CD or a capella.)

O Come All Ye Faithful

Words: John F. Wade, circa 1743. Verses translated by Frederick Oakeley. Music: Adeste Fideles, attributed variously to John Wade, John Reading, or Simao Portogallo.

Alt. music by David LaChance, Jr. © 2014 Sovereign Grace Praise (BMI). Sovereign Grace Music, a division of Sovereign Grace Ministries. All rights reserved. International copyright secured. Administration by Integrity Music.

VERSE 1

O come, all ye faithful, joyful and triumphant
O come ye, O come ye, to Bethlehem
Come and behold Him, born the King of
angels

CHORUS

O come, let us adore Him
O come, let us adore Him
O come, let us adore Him
Christ the Lord

VERSE 2

Yea, Lord, we greet Thee, born this happy
morning
Jesus, to Thee be all glory given
Word of the Father, now in flesh appearing

VERSE 3

True God of true God, Light from Light
Eternal
Humbly, He enters the virgin's womb
Son of the Father, begotten, not created

The Fulfillment of God's Plan: The King Was Crowned with Thorns

SUPPLIES NEEDED:

* piece of purple felt or construction paper

WARM- UP

Bringing Easter and Christmas Together

From a piece of purple felt or construction paper, cut out a cross shape and place it under the baby Jesus in your manger scene. Meanwhile, have someone read John 19:2-6. Then ask your children if they can tell why the purple cross is under the manger. *(Jesus grew up to die on the cross for our sins and rise again to new life on the third day. The Roman soldiers put a purple robe on Jesus and mocked him. When we see the manger, we should always remember Jesus came to save us from our sins.)*

READ THE BIBLE

Light the first, second, and third Advent candles again and then read the Scripture below.

> *And when they came to the place that is called The Skull, there they crucified him, and the criminals, one on his right and one on his left. And Jesus said, "Father, forgive them, for they know not what they do." And they cast lots to divide his garments. And the people stood by, watching, but the rulers scoffed at him, saying, "He saved others; let him save himself, if he is the Christ of God, his Chosen One!" The soldiers also mocked him,*

coming up and offering him sour wine and saying, "If you are the King of the Jews, save yourself!" There was also an inscription over him, "This is the King of the Jews."

One of the criminals who were hanged railed at him, saying, "Are you not the Christ? Save yourself and us!" But the other rebuked him, saying, "Do you not fear God, since you are under the same sentence of condemnation? And we indeed justly, for we are receiving the due reward of our deeds; but this man has done nothing wrong." And he said, "Jesus, remember me when you come into your kingdom." And he said to him, "Truly, I say to you, today you will be with me in Paradise."

It was now about the sixth hour, and there was darkness over the whole land until the ninth hour, while the sun's light failed. And the curtain of the temple was torn in two. Then Jesus, calling out with a loud voice, said, "Father, into your hands I commit my spirit!" And having said this he breathed his last. (Luke 23:33–46)

PICTURE IT

At the start of this week, we read Micah's prophecy, who foretold that a ruler would come from Israel. Jesus was King, but instead of people following him and worshiping him, they mocked him. Jesus was given a purple robe and a crown of thorns. Mocking him, the soldiers said, "Hail, the King of the Jews" (Matthew 27:29). Above his head on the cross, a sign was posted, "This is the King of the Jews." The soldiers didn't realize Jesus was fulfilling all the prophets as he hung on the cross, taking our sin upon himself.

But there was one man, a criminal crucified with Jesus, who believed. He defended Jesus as King, saying, "Jesus, remember me when you come into your kingdom" (Luke 23:42). While the others mocked Jesus, this man, minutes from his own death, believed that Jesus was innocent and destined to reign as King over a heavenly kingdom. Perhaps the robber, moving through the court system that same day, overheard Jesus answer Pilate when he said, "My kingdom is not of this world"

(John 18:36). Or maybe the repentant robber was taught the prophecies of the Bible as a young Jew and now at last believed.

TALK ABOUT IT

Talk with your family about what part of the Christmas message is often forgotten in all the talk about presents, Santa, reindeer, and Christmas trees. *(The message of Jesus is often forgotten in the midst of all that we enjoy about Christmas. We need to be careful that the true meaning of Christmas is never lost, that Christ was born on Christmas day and he grew up to take our punishment on the cross and rise again in victory over death.)*

PRAY TOGETHER

Thank Jesus for leaving heaven to be born as a baby and for growing up to die on the cross for our sins.

SING TOGETHER

(Sing the first song along with the CD or skip to the second song.)

There Blooms a Rose in Bethlehem

Words and Music by Neil DeGraide.

VERSE 1

There blooms a rose in Bethlehem
From tender stem hath sprung
Of Jesse's line this flower grows
As men of old have sung
Isaiah told us long ago
About this rose we'd find
In virgin arms, we shall behold
The Savior of mankind

VERSE 2

The glories of the heavens
Surrounded shepherds bright
The angels sang, a sign was shown
The Christ was born that night

What mystery they came upon
The sign the heralds laud
In manger slept the Holy One
In flesh, the Son of God

VERSE 3

This flow'r in bloom, a scent so sweet
That greets us in the air
It has dispelled with hopefulness
The sting of death's despair
Foretold, this rose was born to die
But would not see decay
So those who place their faith in Him
Shall blossom from the grave

Go, Tell It on the Mountain

Words: John W. Work, Jr., 1907. Music: African-American spiritual.

CHORUS

Go, tell it on the mountain,
Over the hills and everywhere
Go, tell it on the mountain,
That Jesus Christ is born.

VERSE 1

While shepherds kept their watching
O'er silent flocks by night,
Behold, throughout the heavens
There shone a holy light

CHORUS

VERSE 2

The shepherds feared and trembled,

When lo! Above the earth,
Rang out the angel's chorus
That hailed our Savior's birth

CHORUS

VERSE 3

Down in a lowly manger
The humble Christ was born
And God sent us salvation
That blessed Christmas morn.

CHORUS

BARTIMAEUS:
A CHRISTMAS STORY

CHAPTER THREE

Adopted

As the children trooped off to bed, Miss Roberts retreated to her small office, which adjoined the music room. As she closed the door, she slipped her right hand into her skirt pocket where an unopened letter was tucked away. The letter had come the day before and had been shuffled from the office desk to her bedroom dresser and now into her skirt pocket.

Miss Roberts pulled the letter out of her pocket and stood holding it as she tried to muster the courage to read it, hoping against hope for a special Christmas present, the only real Christmas cheer the children of Bartimaeus were likely to have. She took a deep breath, tore the flap, pulled out the letter, and unfolded it while whispering a simple prayer, "Please, please."

She didn't read beyond the first line. It was a rejection; a polite rejection, yes, but a rejection nonetheless. She knew then that Mary would never be adopted.

A few weeks ago Miss Roberts had received word from a couple in the next town expressing an interest in adopting. The couple had a younger child who was blind, and they were looking to adopt an older daughter to help care for him. They didn't say a flat No, it simply said "we're just not ready." But Miss Roberts was experienced enough to know a rejection when she saw one. Heaven knows she had heard enough of them over the years.

"At least I had the good sense not to say anything about it to Mary," she told her empty office, comforting herself some as she slipped the letter back into her pocket and crumpled it with a fist. "Why?" she called out loudly then dropped to her knees. "Why?" she said again, softer this time. Then all at once the tears flowed like a mighty rush from a broken dam. She cried out, pleading desperately, "Please, please, God, she'll be eighteen."

Memories of her own childhood rose unbidden. She recalled how the Sisters of Mercy who helped run Bartimaeus years ago had offered to take her in when she turned eighteen. They needed her help, they told her. But she knew their offer had only been made out of pity and kindness. "And it wasn't the same as a family," she sighed. What the Sisters had offered her was not what she wanted to offer Mary. "God," she cried, "give her a family for Christmas."

The Colonel arrived at ten o'clock sharp the next morning. He offered to direct the choir's practice himself. She had recovered somewhat from the emotional turmoil of the evening before and considered taking her desk work into the library for more privacy, but she was curious to see how the Colonel would deal with the children. She left her office door ajar and listened in on the conversation.

"All right, children," the Colonel's deep voice bellowed above the chatter to command their attention. "Take your places and let's give your song a try." She could hear him taking his seat at the old upright piano. After a spirited introduction to "Joy to the World," he slowed his pace to cue them to begin singing verse one. The children began hesitantly, entering randomly, and singing with little volume or enthusiasm. Miss Roberts cringed. The Colonel abruptly stopped playing.

Miss Roberts rolled her eyes. That poor man. She could only imagine he was finding it hard to believe that anyone could turn "Joy to the World" into a funeral march.

A long moment passed before he broke the silence. "Look," he said, and she could hear him rising from the piano stool. "I happen to know you can sing. Only yesterday, not long before I met with Miss Roberts, I was walking home from the market and cut through the back alley. I thought I heard singing from the Bartimaeus House— that *is* where I am, isn't it?—and I knew you children were in the show. So I walked up to the windows on the other side of your dining hall. Sure enough, you children were singing for your supper. 'A Grueling Life,' I believe you call it?"

Miss Roberts could hear his footfall as he paced the floor in front of them—down and back. Then the Colonel stopped and shouted: "In four-part harmony, at that! That proves one thing to me. You can sing . . . when you want to."

"You're a spy?" one of the younger boys challenged.

"No, I'm not a spy, Bobby," the Colonel told him. "That was a recon mission. But you can think of me as a spy. I know a lot more than you realize."

"Yes, sir," Bobby said.

Miss Roberts cocked her head. Strange. How did he know the boy's name? She was quite certain that the children had not introduced themselves to the Colonel by name. "I've got it!" the Colonel said. "You young ladies and gentlemen sit down and listen for a minute, and then we will give it another try. I just bet it will sound a whole lot different—and let's hope better—the second time around."

I doubt that, thought Miss Roberts. She was still wondering how on earth the Colonel knew Bobby's name. Then again, he was right about the children: They could sing when they wanted to. She had never given it much thought before.

"Let me ask you a question," the Colonel said to pique the children's curiosity. "Who first announced the words to this song, 'Joy to the World'?"

It's not working, Miss Roberts thought as the Colonel's question was met with silence.

The Colonel said, "Say, did you know that this song is about adoption?"

Murmurs rose and echoed in the room. Miss Roberts could hear the children shuffling their feet. Now he had their attention. Every orphan perked up at the very mention of the word *adoption.* Of course they didn't believe "Joy to the World" was about adoption, but he definitely had their attention.

Mary broke the silence. "So how is 'Joy to the World' about adoption?" she asked obligingly.

"Well, I'm glad you asked," the Colonel replied. "Let me tell you the story of this great song. Listen carefully and then see if you can figure out for yourself how it's a song about adoption."

The suspense was building. Even Miss Roberts laid her paperwork aside, rolled her chair up to the door, and put her ear to the crack.

"Well, it starts with the Christmas story. You know how the story goes: Certain shepherds were watching their flocks by night." The Colonel paused for a moment and she could hear him sitting back down on the piano stool. "Suddenly, an angel of the Lord appeared to them and the glory of the Lord shown all about them. At first, the shepherds were terrified, but the angel told them not to be afraid, saying, 'I bring you good news of great joy that will be for all people.' That, my dear children, is where the song 'Joy to the World' gets its name. The angel brought a message of joy—to—the—world. Get it? The angel told them that a very special baby had been born in Bethlehem and was lying in a manger, wrapped in swaddling clothes."

"Hey that's the baby Jesus," Christopher shouted.

"That's right," the Colonel answered.

The Colonel continued. "Then, when the angel finished making the announcement the heavens opened and thousands of angels began to sing. The song 'Joy to the World' celebrates the angel's announcement of good news and great joy for all people."

"OK, that explains the joy part, but Jesus wasn't an orphan," Timothy objected.

"You are certainly right about that Timothy," the Colonel agreed. "Jesus was not an orphan. But he was adopted, right?"

"Huh?"

"Joseph wasn't his father."

The children's voices rose in a collective "Ahhh."

Miss Roberts leaned back in her chair thoughtfully. She had never thought of Jesus as adopted before.

The Colonel continued. "You see, children, Jesus's real father was God himself. When Jesus was born, Joseph cared for him as his very own son. So you see, Jesus was adopted!"

"OK, Colonel," Timothy admitted, "you got us on that one. So . . . joy to the world, it's Christmas time," he said with a touch of sarcasm. "Look, I don't mean to be disrespectful, but take a look around you. We started the year with thirty-two orphans. It is now December 23. Do the math yourself. We don't have thirty-two orphans now—we have thirty-three. No offense, Colonel, but it seems like things are going in the wrong direction."

"Does it seem so?" the Colonel asked.

Timothy said, "You see, there isn't much joy to go around these days. Some might think it looks a bit drab around here for Christmas, but Miss Roberts is right. There's no use putting on a show. And that is just what we would be doing if we sang your song all peppy-like. There are no adoptions sitting under the Christmas tree this year."

Silence.

Though Miss Roberts didn't approve of Timothy's disrespect, she found herself agreeing with him. So what if Jesus was adopted? That wasn't going to help the children this Christmas.

"That's where you're wrong, Timmy," the Colonel said. "You're wondering how I know your name, aren't you? Your given name is Timothy, but everyone calls you Timmy. So I will, too. I know you all by name," the Colonel said. Then, one by one, he rattled off all of their names.

Miss Roberts was astounded, and so were the children.

"You are all wrong," he continued. "God has adoption papers ready for each one of you. They're just waiting for you to pick them up. And you don't have to wait until Christmas."

The children didn't know what to say. Miss Roberts was confused and annoyed. She was tempted to go in and put an end to the Colonel's fairy tales, but she stayed put, curious to see where he was going with this.

"That's right, adoption papers," the Colonel repeated. "Let me explain. Jesus didn't stay a baby in a manger, you know. Later, when he was a man, he left his home on a very special mission for God the Father. John the Baptist, Jesus's cousin, announced the start of his ministry. He called Jesus the Lamb of God who would take away the sins of the world.

"Jesus gave blind people sight, fed thousands with a small basket of food, and even raised people back to life. Most importantly, Jesus called all the people to turn away from their sins and follow him.

"There were those, however, who didn't like being called sinners. These people killed Jesus. But Jesus willingly took our sin and the punishment we deserved so that all who place their trust in him could be forgiven."

The Colonel paused for a moment and utter silence filled the room. Then he continued. "Jesus died, but after three days, he came back to life. Now, God promises that all who turn away from their sin and believe in Jesus will be forgiven. Each one of us is a sinner, you know, and it only takes one sin to separate you from God—one lie, one angry word, one bad thought. But if you trust in Jesus, God will wash all your sins away."

Miss Roberts sat with her chin in her hands listening.

"And here's the very best part. God says in the Bible that all those who place their trust in Jesus are adopted into God's family. Look, kids, you've been through a lot. I know you have and my heart breaks for each and every one of you. Most of you have never known a father. But listen: If you trust Jesus, God becomes your Father, and in that moment you're not an orphan any more, you're adopted."

Christopher shouted, "I knew there was a special reason for putting that baby in the manger. Look, guys, the Colonel is right. I admit that even I couldn't believe how bad you were singing. If you—I mean we—can sing like a canary for a bowl of porridge, then why not sing 'Joy to the World' with a little more zip?"

"He's right," one of the girls said, and the other children broke into a chorus of agreement, and a newfound excitement spread through their ranks.

Meanwhile over in the office, Miss Roberts was shell-shocked. Somewhere in the midst of the Colonel's presentation, God reached down and opened her eyes. No one had ever explained the Christmas story like that. She knew about the baby Jesus and the shepherds, but she didn't know he grew up to be a Savior—her Savior. Now she was on her knees, crying tears of joy. The Spirit of God had filled her heart just about the time the Colonel explained the part about never being an orphan again. In mere seconds, years of bitterness began to melt away.

Quietly while on her knees, she dared to say the words she thought would never pass her lips. "I'm adopted," she said, in a whisper at first. Then she said it again, and again, louder and louder, until finally she was shouting. "I'm adopted! I'm adopted! I'm adopted!" The whole street might have heard and thought she was crazy if it were not for thirty-three orphans singing "Joy to the World" at the top of their lungs—in unison.

Miss Roberts stood in the hall and looked in at the children as they sang. When the Colonel finally signaled them to close, none of the children wanted to stop. But they followed his lead as he raised his hands directing their great crescendo. Then, as he brought down his hands sharply they stopped, and not one child missed the cue.

The Colonel closed his eyes to savor the moment, then he smiled and said, "Every year the children of this orphanage sing 'Joy to the World' for the YMCA Community Christmas Concert. From what the cook tells me, for the last five years there's been less and less joy in your song. I have a feeling that this year will be different."

The children cheered. Miss Roberts was completely undone. All these years she had been discouraging the children instead of building their faith. No wonder the adoptions had all but dried up. She had blamed it on the war. *Not anymore*, she thought to herself. *There will be Christmas at Bartimaeus!*

God's Promise: Salvation Will Come through My Servant

WARM-UP

Your Best Christmas Gift

Have everyone share what they believe was the best present they ever received for Christmas. Make sure that the grown-ups participate too. After everyone is finished, remind your children that the best Christmas gift of all was God sending his Son Jesus, as a baby in a manger. When we give our gifts on Christmas, we should do so remembering that on Christmas, God gave us the best gift of all—his only Son. Our gift giving should be patterned after God's, who gave his only Son to die on the cross for our sins.

READ THE BIBLE

Light all the Advent candles except for the one in the middle and then read the Scripture below.

Behold my servant, whom I uphold, my chosen, in whom my soul delights; I have put my Spirit upon him; he will bring forth justice to the nations. He will not cry aloud or lift up his voice, or make it heard in the street; a bruised reed he will not break, and a faintly burning wick he will not quench; he will faithfully bring forth justice. He will not grow faint or be discouraged till he has established justice in the earth; and the coastlands wait for his law. Thus says God, the LORD, who created the heavens and stretched them out, who spread out the earth and what comes from it, who gives breath to the people on it and spirit to those

who walk in it: "I am the LORD; I have called you in righteous-
ness; I will take you by the hand and keep you; I will give you as
a covenant for the people, a light for the nations, to open the
eyes that are blind, to bring out the prisoners from the dungeon,
from the prison those who sit in darkness." (Isaiah 42:1-7)

PICTURE IT

Isaiah's prophecies are so amazing that, at one time, many people claimed the book of Isaiah was a fake. They found it hard to believe that anyone could have foretold so perfectly what was going to happen to Jesus. How could anyone get so many details right and know that the Messiah would be born of a virgin, both man and God, open the eyes of the blind, and die, crushed for the sins of God's people? The book of Isaiah, they charged, must have been written after Jesus was born. Then, in 1947, the Dead Sea Scrolls were discovered in a cave. Among the parchments found in clay jars was a complete scroll of the book of Isaiah. When it was scientifically tested to see how old it was, it dated back to 100 years before Jesus was born, proving the book of Isaiah was not a fake.

Isaiah prophesied that the Lord's chosen servant will "open the eyes that are blind" (Isaiah 42:7), and "not grow faint or be discouraged till he has established justice in the earth" (42:4). We can be sure God spoke through Isaiah. God's promises are trustworthy and true. Jesus was born of a virgin (7:14), became a king in the line of David (Isaiah 9:7), had God's Spirit rest on him (11:2), was crushed for our sin (Isaiah 53:5), was buried in a rich man's tomb (53:9), and because he rose again from the dead will return to judge the earth (11:4-5).

TALK ABOUT IT

Ask, "How did a man like Isaiah write prophecies about Jesus hundreds of years before Jesus was even born?" *(While the books of the Bible, like the book of Isaiah, were written by men, God tells us in 2 Timothy 3:16 that Scripture is "breathed out by God." So, much like when we write a letter we use a pencil or pen, God wrote the*

Bible using people like Isaiah. The Spirit of God helped them know what to write. That's how Isaiah could write about Jesus, long before he was born.)

PRAY TOGETHER
Thank God for his amazing Word and ask him to help you grow in your love for his Word and in your desire to read it.

SING TOGETHER
(Sing the first song along with the CD or skip to the second song.)

The Unbelievable
Words and Music by Steve and Vikki Cook.

VERSE 1
Come and see the inconceivable
And believe the unbelievable
God has come to dwell with us
Begotten Son born into Adam's earth
Promised One fulfilling ancient words
God has come to dwell with us

VERSE 2
He will heal the unhealable
He will save the unsavable
God has come to dwell with us
Heaven's joy will drink our bitter cup
Emptied out as He is lifted up
God has come to dwell with us

BRIDGE
Who could ever know the depths
Of the myst'ry of Your grace?
Though our minds can't take it in
Lord, our hearts are filled with praise

VERSE 3
Lord we're lost in overwhelming awe
At the thought of this amazing love
God has come, God has come
God has come to dwell with us

The First Noel
Traditional English carol, seventeenth century.

VERSE 1
The first Noel the angels did say
Was to certain poor shepherds in fields as
  they lay;
In fields where they lay, keeping their sheep,
On a cold winter's night that was so deep:

CHORUS
Noel, Noel, Noel, Noel

Born is the King of Israel.

VERSE 2
They looked up and saw a star,
Shining in the east, beyond them far:
And to the earth it gave great light,
And so it continued both day and night:

CHORUS

Simeon's Announcement: Welcomed at the Temple

SUPPLIES NEEDED:

* string of Christmas lights
* drawing paper
* pencils, crayons, or colored pencils

WARM-UP

—Plug in a string of Christmas lights. Talk about the lights with your children. Ask them why we have Christmas lights. Ask them to name some things that light is good for.

—Read John 8:12a: "Again Jesus spoke to them, saying, 'I am the light of the world.'"

—Ask your children if they have any idea why Jesus called himself the "light of the world."

—After they offer their suggestions, read John 8:12b: "Whoever follows me will not walk in darkness, but will have the light of life."

—Talk together about what it means to "walk in darkness" and then what it means to "have the light of life."

READ THE BIBLE

Light all the Advent candles again except for the one in the middle and then read the Scripture below.

Now there was a man in Jerusalem, whose name was Simeon, and this man was righteous and devout, waiting for the consolation of Israel, and the Holy Spirit was upon him. And it had been revealed to him by the Holy Spirit that he would not see death before he had seen the Lord's Christ. And he came in the Spirit into the temple, and when the parents brought in the child Jesus, to do for him according to the custom of the Law, he took him up in his arms and blessed God and said, "Lord, now you are letting your servant depart in peace, according to your word; for my eyes have seen your salvation that you have prepared in the presence of all peoples, a light for revelation to the Gentiles, and for glory to your people Israel."

And his father and his mother marveled at what was said about him. And Simeon blessed them and said to Mary his mother, "Behold, this child is appointed for the fall and rising of many in Israel, and for a sign that is opposed (and a sword will pierce through your own soul also), so that thoughts from many hearts may be revealed." (Luke 2:25-35)

PICTURE IT

Simeon studied the Bible and believed God's promise to rescue his people by sending a savior. What is more amazing is that God promised Simeon that he would get to see the Messiah before he died. One day, the Holy Spirit led Simeon to the temple to meet the Savior. He must have been so excited as he watched each person arrive. When Mary and Joseph brought Jesus, Simeon knew the baby she held gently in her arms was the one God would raise up to rule his people.

Simeon took the baby Jesus in his arms, knowing that he held the Savior of the world. Filled with the Holy Spirit, he confirmed the words of Isaiah, that Jesus would become a "light for the nations" (Isaiah 42:6).

Like Isaiah, Simeon foretold of Christ's suffering, confirming that Jesus would have enemies, his life would divide the nation, and there would be a time of great sadness for Mary. Simeon's words all came true. Jesus was rejected by the religious rulers, who plotted his murder (John 11:53) and crucified him. Mary's soul was pierced as she watched her son die upon the cross. Yet that was not the end of the story. Mary survived those sorrows and lived to celebrate the rising of her son Jesus (Acts 1:14) and witness the light of the gospel going to the nations.

TALK ABOUT IT

Ask, "What did Isaiah (and later Simeon) mean by calling Jesus a light to the nations?" *(Sin is described in the Bible as darkness. God is described as light for he has no sin [1 John 1:5]. By calling Jesus a light, they were letting us know that Jesus was more than a man; he was God and he came to bring God's light to us. His death on the cross made it possible for our sins to be forgiven and those who believe to become the light of the world with him [John 8:12].)*

PRAY TOGETHER

Praise Jesus as ruler over all the nations. Declare that everyone must bow before our great king.

SING TOGETHER

(Sing the first song along with the CD or skip to the second song.)

Prepare Him Room

Words and Music by Rebecca Elliott and Dave Fournier.

VERSE 1
O behold, the mystery now unfolds
See the star shine on the virgin foretold
Angels sing and light up the sky
Hope rings out in a newborn's cry
Swing wide, you ancient gates
For Christ is born today!

CHORUS
Prepare him room
Prepare him room
Let the King of glory enter in

VERSE 2
God with us, the promise has come to be

This, the one the prophets were longing to see
In the darkness a blazing light
To the hungry the words of life
His kingdom now is near
For those with ears to hear

VERSE 3
Oh, our hearts, as busy as Bethlehem
Hear Him knock, don't say there's no room in the inn
Through the cradle, cross, and grave
See the love of God displayed
Now He's risen and he reigns
Praise the Name above all names!

Good Christian Men Rejoice

Words: Heinrich Suso (?-1366); translated from Latin to English by John M. Neale (1853). Music: In Dulci Jubilo, 14th Century German melody (1871).

VERSE 1

Good Christian men rejoice
With heart and soul and voice!
Give ye heed to what we say
News! News!
Jesus Christ is born today!
Ox and ass before Him bow
And He is in the manger now
Christ is born today!
Christ is born today!

VERSE 2

Good Christian men, rejoice
With heart and soul and voice
Now ye hear of endless bliss
Joy! Joy!

Jesus Christ was born for this
He hath open'd the heav'nly door
And man is blessed evermore
Christ was born for this
Christ was born for this

VERSE 3

Good Christian men, rejoice
With heart and soul and voice
Now ye need not fear the grave:
Peace! Peace!
Jesus Christ was born to save
Calls you one and calls you all
To gain His everlasting hall
Christ was born to save
Christ was born to save

ACTIVITY

Draw the Scene

Work together as a family to draw a picture of Joseph and Mary with Jesus in her arms, and Simeon standing nearby with his hands raised in praise to God. At the bottom of the page, write the words "A Light to the Nations." Explain to your children that the Gentiles Simeon talked about really represent the other peoples of the world (those who are not Jewish), and that is what Isaiah meant when he prophesied the Messiah would be a "light to the nations." That is why we can reach out to all our neighbors no matter what country or people they came from.

The Fulfillment of God's Plan: People from Every Nation around the Throne

SUPPLIES NEEDED:

* ✳ one sheet 8 1/2" x 11" paper
* ✳ pinch sand (or salt)
* ✳ ingredients for cookies (see activity on p. 69)

WARM-UP

Try and Count the Sand

Sprinkle a very small pinch of sand on a sheet of white paper and have your children count the grains one by one. You may be surprised to see the large number of grains of sand in just one pinch. Now help your children imagine all the grains of sand on the seashore. The Bible tells us there will be such a multitude of people in heaven that no one will be able to count them (Revelation 7:9)! Heaven will be full of believers, from every nation and from every age.

READ THE BIBLE

Light all the Advent candles again except for the one in the middle and then read the Scripture below.

> *After this I looked, and behold, a great multitude that no one could number, from every nation, from all tribes and peoples and languages, standing before the throne and before the*

Lamb, clothed in white robes, with palm branches in their hands, and crying out with a loud voice, "Salvation belongs to our God who sits on the throne, and to the Lamb!" And all the angels were standing around the throne and around the elders and the four living creatures, and they fell on their faces before the throne and worshiped God, saying, "Amen! Blessing and glory and wisdom and thanksgiving and honor and power and might be to our God forever and ever! Amen."
(Revelation 7:9–12)

PICTURE IT

God's plan to reach the nations, first revealed to Abraham (Genesis 18:18), then prophesied by Isaiah (Isaiah 42:6), and then announced by Simeon (Luke 2:32), is fulfilled when Jesus returns in the end. We get a sneak peak at the last chapter of the story by reading the vision God gave to the apostle John. John wrote down what he saw and called it "The Revelation of Jesus Christ," which is the last book in the Bible.

God told Abraham that he would be a blessing to the nations and that his offspring would be as numerous as the sand on the seashore (Genesis 32:12). Now, in today's reading we see the fulfillment of that word, as people from every nation, more than anyone could count, are standing before the throne, crying out to Jesus the Lamb, "Salvation belongs to our God who sits on the throne" (Revelation 7:10).

All of us who believe and trust in Jesus will one day be a part of this great multitude. Gabriel, who delivered God's announcement to Mary, will be there. The angel of the Lord who spoke to Joseph in a dream, along with the angels who announced the birth of Jesus to the shepherds will all be there. We'll see Simeon, who announced the arrival of God's Messiah at the temple—John, Elizabeth, Mary, Joseph, and even the repentant thief on the cross. All the prophets, like Micah and Isaiah, will celebrate with us. With one voice we will all shout "Salvation belongs to our God who sits on the throne, and unto the Lamb!" We will proclaim with all our might, "To him who sits on the throne and to the Lamb be blessing and honor and glory and might forever and ever!" (Revelation 5:13).

TALK ABOUT IT

Give everyone a chance to pick someone from this Advent study that they are looking forward to seeing in heaven. *(Of course we will all look forward to seeing Jesus, but try to prompt your children to think of some of the Bible characters we learned about, like the prophet Isaiah, the angel Gabriel, or Mary and Joseph.)*

PRAY TOGETHER

Pray the words from Revelation: "To him who sits on the throne and to the Lamb be blessing and honor and glory and might forever and ever!" *(Then have everyone shout "Amen!")*

SING TOGETHER

(Sing along with the CD or a capella.)

Hark! The Herald Angels Sing

Words by Charles Wesley (1739). Music: MENDELSSOHN, Felix Mendelssohn.

VERSE 1

Hark! The herald angels sing
"Glory to the newborn King
Peace on earth, and mercy mild
God and sinners reconciled!"
Joyful, all ye nations rise
Join the triumph of the skies
With th'angelic host proclaim
"Christ is born in Bethlehem!"

CHORUS

Hark! the herald angels sing
"Glory to the newborn King!"

VERSE 2

Christ, by highest Heav'n adored
Christ, the everlasting Lord

Late in time, behold Him come
Offspring of a virgin's womb
Veiled in flesh the Godhead see
Hail th'incarnate Deity
Pleased as man with man to dwell
Jesus, our Emmanuel

VERSE 3

Hail the heav'n-born Prince of Peace!
Hail the Sun of Righteousness!
Light and life to all He brings
Ris'n with healing in His wings
Mild He lays His glory by
Born that man no more may die
Born to raise the sons of earth
Born to give them second birth

ACTIVITY

Bake some Christmas cookies together. Below are two recipes to get you started. You'll find a reference to the second recipe in this week's installment of the Bartimaeus story.

Emma's Butterscotch Holiday Cookies

These cookies are a special part of the Machowski Christmas. Every year my wife Lois mixes up a batch. After the dough is chilled, we roll it out and cut out a whole variety of Christmas cookies, from reindeer to snowmen. Once they finish baking and cool, we gather around the table with all kinds of sprinkles and frosting to decorate them. Make a few plates of the decorated cookies to give away to your neighbors as a Christmas gift.

Ingredients:

2 1/2 cups all-purpose flour
1 teaspoon baking powder
1/8 teaspoon baking soda
1/4 teaspoon salt
3/4 cup butter, softened
1 cup light brown sugar, packed
1 teaspoon vanilla
1 egg, well beaten

1. Sift flour with baking powder, baking soda, and salt.

2. Cream butter until light; add sugar gradually, beating until fluffy; then add vanilla and egg and beat until smooth.

3. Add sifted dry ingredients gradually, beating well after each addition.

4. Gather dough into ball and flatten into disk. Wrap in plastic and chill until firm, at least 4 hours.

5. Roll dough 1/8-inch thick on a lightly floured surface.

6. Cut cookies out with your favorite Christmas cookie cutters, lay on an ungreased cookie sheet

7. Bake in a hot oven, preheated to 450 degrees for about 6 minutes.

8. Decorate with your favorite frosting and sugary sprinkles.

Mrs. Schultz's Christmas Ginger Cookies

Join the Christmas tradition of the children of Bartimaeus by making a batch of Mrs. Schultz's special Christmas ginger cookies, wrapped in wax paper, and placed under the tree for a Christmas Eve treat. Give out the cookies from youngest to oldest, sing "Joy to the World," then open up your cookies and enjoy!

Ingredients:
6 cups all-purpose flour
1 tablespoon baking powder
1 tablespoon ground ginger
1 1/4 teaspoon ground cloves
1 teaspoon ground nutmeg
1 teaspoon ground cinnamon
1 cup shortening, melted and cooled slightly
1 cup molasses
1 cup packed brown sugar
1/2 cup water 1 egg
1 teaspoon vanilla extract

1. Mix together the flour, baking powder, ginger, cloves, nutmeg, and cinnamon; set aside.

2. In a large bowl, mix together the shortening, molasses, brown sugar, water, egg, and vanilla until smooth. Gradually stir in the dry ingredients completely. Divide dough into 3 pieces, flattening each into a 1 1/2-inch thick disk, wrap in plastic wrap, and refrigerate for a minimum of 3 hours.

3. Preheat oven to 350 degrees F (175 degrees C). On a lightly floured surface, roll the dough out to 1/4-inch thickness. Cut into circles with a glass or desired shapes with cookie cutters. Place cookies 1 inch apart onto an ungreased cookie sheet.

4. Bake for 10 to 12 minutes in the preheated oven. When the cookies are done, they will look dry, but still be soft to the touch. Remove from the baking sheet to cool on wire racks. When cool, the cookies can be frosted with the icing of your choice. Let frosting harden.

5. Wrap 5 cookies in wax paper for each person in your family and tie them up with a ribbon and a small name tag and place the cookies under your Christmas tree.

BARTIMAEUS:
A CHRISTMAS STORY

CHAPTER FOUR

Christmas Returns to Bartimaeus

While the children finished up their practice with the Colonel, Miss Roberts formulated a plan. Mrs. Schultz was the perfect person to help her. She pulled herself together and entered the music room.

"Well done, Colonel," she said, clearing her throat and standing as stiffly as she could to hide her emotion. "If I didn't hear it myself, I wouldn't have believed the transformation. If you'll excuse me."

Then, before the Colonel could reply, she was off to the kitchen.

The next day was Christmas Eve. All through the day as they went about their normal activities, the children hummed "Joy to the World."

When the time to leave drew near, Mrs. Schultz ran to the stairs and called for the children to come. As soon as they heard it was time, an army of excited children rushed down the hallway to the front door, nearly trampling her on the way!

"Where is Miss Roberts?" one of them asked.

"She'll be coming along. The Colonel has agreed to walk you over. Miss Roberts and I will meet you later for the show. Since the Colonel is directing your song, there's no need for us to come early for the warm-up." No sooner had she finished her sentence than a knock at the door signaled it was time to go.

As soon as the last child exited the door, Mrs. Schultz ran back to the kitchen. There was still so much work to do! She flew about the kitchen energized by the real joy that had come over the house. It wasn't long before she was wrapping the last of the ginger cookies in waxed paper packets tied with string.

Though all of the performances at the Community Christmas Show were wonderful, the children from Bartimaeus stole the show. There was a contagious joy in their voices. Their spirited version of "Joy to the World" was the perfect close for the program. At the final crescendo, the audience rose to their feet and, the moment they were done, broke out in a thunderous ovation. As the applause died down, some people asked, "Where did these children come from?" While others, regular attendees at the annual event, asked themselves and each other if these were the same children from Bartimaeus who had performed at the show the previous year.

In the audience, Miss Roberts nodded to Mrs. Schultz. A minute later they had slipped out unnoticed.

The Colonel walked up the steps and took the stage. "May God give all of you joy in this Christmas season," he started. "Thank you, children," he said, turning and giving a warm smile and nod to the Bartimaeus children. At once, the whole audience again erupted in spontaneous applause. "Some of these children," he said, "have spent many a Christmas at Bartimaeus. I want to ask you a favor. This Christmas, please, let's all keep them in mind. All around our great city are couples without children who might love to adopt a child. They simply don't know what a great bunch of kids we have right here at Bartimaeus." Continuing, he said, "As we enjoy this season, let's pray that this is the last Christmas any one of these children need spend without a family. And may God bring the war to a close. Thank you all for coming. May the joy of the Lord go with you as we celebrate the birth of our Savior. Merry Christmas." He brought the show to a close and was met with yet more joyful applause.

As they exited their seats everyone talked about the children and what a wonderful night it had been, and it was some time before everyone left. Many took an opportunity to greet the Bartimaeus children one by one.

Back at the orphanage, Miss Roberts went to her room, and Mrs. Schultz went to the kitchen and pulled two large bowls off the counter. She stacked one on top of the other with a breadboard in between. She then carried them to the music room and lit the candles, working as fast as she could without burning the place to the ground! Suddenly, she heard a scream from the direction of Miss Roberts's room. She stopped what she was doing and ran down the hall and up the stairs. Out of breath by the time she reached Miss Roberts's room, she paused for a second before pushing open the door.

"How silly of me! I didn't read the whole letter," Miss Roberts exclaimed. "I didn't read the whole letter!"

"What letter? Are you all right?" Mrs. Schultz asked, puzzled.

"Now just listen to this Christmas present, will you?" Miss Roberts slowly read aloud the letter she had crumpled and almost thrown in the trash. "Dear Miss Roberts," she began, holding back tears. "I'm sorry to disappoint you, but we won't be ready to pursue the adoption until after Christmas. But we are so excited about Mary. Please call us after the holidays. We hope this letter and our eager acceptance of your offer to adopt Mary will serve to provide the Christmas present you were hoping to give her. We see her as an answer to our prayers. Merry Christmas, the Stetson family."

By the time she finished reading the letter both of the women were jumping up and down. When at last they came to their senses, they stared at each other, and after a brief pause, shouted together, "The children!" Without another word, both women scrambled down the stairs and resumed working at lightning speed. Just as they finished, they heard voices on the porch outside. Miss Roberts said as she walked briskly to the door and paused for a moment to put a stern expression on her face. Opening the door a crack and peeking out, she said gruffly, "You're late."

Some of the children dropped their heads, but the Colonel, standing at the top of the stairs, gave Miss Roberts a wink and said, "Charge the fault to my account. We had to wait till every last person was greeted and gone. I am the director, you know."

"Well, shake off your boots and come in before you catch cold," she said and then turned away from the door. When all the children had clambered into the foyer, Miss Roberts told them to never mind their wet feet and follow her. Miss Roberts moved quickly down the hallway toward the music room. She couldn't help but crack a smile as she moved at a faster pace than usual to stay a step ahead of the children. She disappeared ahead of them into the room.

"Here I am walking back in here with wet shoes!" Christopher whispered loudly. "Sound familiar?"

"Welcome back to the dungeon," Timothy replied, loud enough for Christopher to hear. "The imperfect end to an imperfect evening," he said.

But as soon as Timothy, Christopher, and the other children turned the corner they could not believe their eyes. The whole room was decorated . . . decorated for Christmas!

"A tree, a real live Christmas tree!" one of the boys shouted.

"With popcorn and cranberry garland," another added.

"Look!" shouted one of the girls pointing under the tree. "It's a manger. A manger under the tree!"

"But where is the baby?" another of the girls asked as she bent down to look.

"Christopher," Miss Roberts called, "I believe this is your job." Then she handed him a handcarved wooden box.

"I can't believe it," Christopher said. "I must be dreaming." He blinked his eyes several times as if to be sure. Convinced it was all

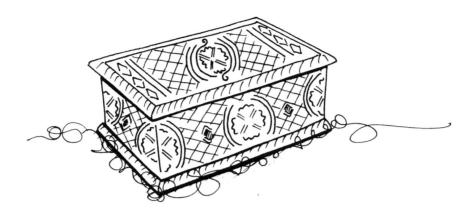

really happening, instinctively he opened the box and carefully lifted out the porcelain infant. He bent down and placed the baby Jesus into the manger. Then he looked left, "Timothy," he ordered with excitement, "bring over the shepherds!" Timothy didn't miss a beat and moved the shepherds close to the manger. "Mary," he continued, turning to the right. "Bring over the wise men."

When they were through, Miss Roberts addressed the children. "In most homes it is a tradition to wait till Christmas morning to open Christmas gifts. But I can't wait." She shouted, "So, from this day forward, all presents at Bartimaeus will be opened on Christmas Eve!"

The children whooped and hollered as they only now noticed the paper wrapped packages, each tied with a bow tucked under the tree.

"There is a gift for each of you," she said. "But before you open them, I have two very special announcements to make." Miss Roberts raised her hands palms out to settle them down. "First, you may be wondering what is going on. Especially those of you who have been here for a while." She paused for a moment to fight back the tears. "Well, yesterday, while the Colonel was here to help you with your song I was listening too. Yesterday, children, I was adopted . . . by God!" A tear rolled down her cheek, but she held herself together. "And, Mary, this is announcement number two. This one is for you. Can you read it to the children?" she said as she handed the crumpled letter to Mary.

The children watched and waited eagerly, but Mary only cried. Once she regained her composure enough to read her letter out loud, there was no doubting the Christmas celebration that evening at Bartimaeus. Everyone danced and shouted and the children had to be reminded to open their gifts.

Each one received a packet of Mrs. Schultz's best ginger cookies. As the children finished opening their gifts, the Colonel touched Miss Roberts's arm lightly. As she turned, he said, "Well done, Elizabeth," and started singing: "Joy to the world, the Lord is come . . ." The children all joined in, and if possible, outdid their concert performance.

The Great War ended that next year before Christmas and the director of the YMCA returned in June. The Colonel stayed on to help Elizabeth Roberts place the children in good homes. Mary was the first to leave Bartimaeus just a few days into the New Year, months ahead of her eighteenth birthday. By the next Christmas none of the orphans remained; all had been adopted into loving families. They all left Bartimaeus, all except one. Christopher remained there. But he too was adopted, by Colonel Bart Jackson II—that is Bartimaeus Jackson—and his new bride Elizabeth. Orphans still passed through Bartimaeus but their stays were short, a brief pause on the way to a new family. And if any were fortunate enough to stay over for Christmas, they opened their gifts early, just after the concert on Christmas Eve.

The Fulfillment of God's Plan: Christ Is Born!

CHRISTMAS DAY SCRIPTURE READING

Light all the Advent candles and read the story of Jesus's birth from Luke 2.

In those days a decree went out from Caesar Augustus that all the world should be registered. This was the first registration when Quirinius was governor of Syria. And all went to be registered, each to his own town. And Joseph also went up from Galilee, from the town of Nazareth, to Judea, to the city of David, which is called Bethlehem, because he was of the house and lineage of David, to be registered with Mary, his betrothed, who was with child. And while they were there, the time came for her to give birth. And she gave birth to her firstborn son and wrapped him in swaddling cloths and laid him in a manger, because there was no place for them in the inn.

And in the same region there were shepherds out in the field, keeping watch over their flock by night. And an angel of the Lord appeared to them, and the glory of the Lord shone around them, and they were filled with great fear. And the angel said to them, "Fear not, for behold, I bring you good news of great joy that will be for all the people. For unto you is born this day in the city of David a Savior, who is Christ the Lord. And this will be a sign for you: you will find a baby wrapped in swaddling cloths and lying in a manger." And suddenly there was with the angel a multitude of the heavenly host praising God and saying, "Glory to God in the highest, and on earth peace among those with whom he is pleased!"

When the angels went away from them into heaven, the shepherds said to one another, "Let us go over to Bethlehem and see this thing that has happened, which the Lord has made known to us." And they went with haste and found Mary and Joseph, and the baby lying in a manger. And when they saw it, they made known the saying that had been told them concerning this child. And all who heard it wondered at what the shepherds told them. But Mary treasured up all these things, pondering them in her heart. And the shepherds returned, glorifying and praising God for all they had heard and seen, as it had been told them. (Luke 2:1-20)

SING TOGETHER
(Sing along with the CD or a capella.)

Joy to the World

Words: Isaac Watts (1719). Music: ANTIOCH, arranged by Lowell Mason. Additional words and music by David LaChance, Jr.

VERSE 1
Joy to the world! the Lord is come
Let earth receive her King
Let every heart prepare Him room
And heaven and nature sing
And heaven and nature sing
And heaven, and heaven, and nature sing

VERSE 2
Joy to the world! the Savior reigns
Let men their songs employ
While fields and floods, rocks, hills, and plains
Repeat the sounding joy
Repeat the sounding joy
Repeat, repeat the sounding joy

VERSE 3
No more let sins and sorrows grow
Nor thorns infest the ground
He comes to make His blessings flow
Far as the curse is found
Far as the curse is found
Far as, far as, the curse is found

VERSE 4
He rules the world with truth and grace
And makes the nations prove
The glories of His righteousness
And wonders of His love
And wonders of His love
And wonders, wonders, of His love

Let heaven and nature sing

Our God reigns

PRAY TOGETHER

Thank God for sending his Son Jesus into the world as a baby who would one day die on the cross for the forgiveness of our sins. Thank him that all who trust in Jesus will live with him forever and ever in heaven.

 Marty
Machowski

A Unique Program Connecting Children to the Gospel Story
from Genesis to Revelation

Three-year 156 story, Sunday school curriculum for preschool through upper elementary.

Two companion family devotionals, *Long Story Short* (OT) and *Old Story New* (NT) that follow the same 156 stories as the Sunday school curriculum and reinforce the gospel story at home.

An illustrated Bible storybook, *The Gospel Story Bible,* highlights the same 156 stories for churches and families.